DESIFIED

Delicious Recipes for Ramadan, Eid & Every Day

ZAYNAH DIN

DESIFIED

Delicious Recipes for Ramadan, Eid & Every Day

ZAYNAH DIN

Interlink Books

An imprint of Interlink Publishing Group, Inc.
Northampton, Massachusetts

To Mum, the superwoman who taught me how to make round rotis, chicken biryani, and everything in between.

CONTENTS

To **DESI**FY is to elevate foods by infusing them with South Asian flavors and spices.

INTRODUCTION

I grew up eating spaghetti keema instead of spaghetti bolognese. It was always rice in my lunchbox, never sandwiches and chips. My palate was being Desified from the get-go! Desi is a term used to describe people, food, and products of the Indian subcontinent. Desi or Deshi is derived from Sanskrit, and literally means "land," though the word is widely understood to refer to the people of Pakistan, India, and Bangladesh.

I spent most of my childhood following my Pakistani mom around the kitchen—sometimes helping her make rotis, sometimes on rice-washing duty, but most of the time just hoping she would let me taste some meat from the pot. Spending all this time with her allowed me to understand the true essence of Pakistani food.

I became obsessed with experimenting in the kitchen, watching cooking shows, simply eating and enjoying food. I was known in my family and at school as the baker/chef. I held many bake sales through school and college, which eventually led me to create my Instagram @ZaynahsBakes, where I shared cake recipes online. I began to receive messages from people in my local area asking to buy cakes and cupcakes for birthday parties, and my Instagram page quickly transformed into a local home sale cupcake delivery business. Over time I began sharing more and more authentic Pakistani recipes and fusion recipes for Ramadan.

The success of my Ramadan Recipe series allowed me to reach new audiences, the majority of whom are Desi foodies. I continued sharing family-friendly recipes, fusion, and authentic Desi food that anyone can cook and enjoy.

Ramadan is a month of prayer, mindfulness, charity, sharing, and of course fasting. It's an opportunity to get closer to God, to ask for forgiveness, and test our discipline. Suhoor (or Sehri) is the meal we eat before sunrise to prepare ourselves for the day of fasting ahead. It's important to fuel our bodies with long-lasting carbohydrates, protein to keep us as strong as possible, and water so that we are hydrated. Iftar is the evening meal that marks the breaking of our fast. Once the sun has set, we can enjoy food and drink normally until the sun rises again. Dates are significant during Ramadan: it is Sunnah (good habitual

Islamic practice) to break our fast by eating a date, as our Prophet Muhammad (SWT, which is a shorthand way to say, "Glory to Him, the Exalted") did. Dates are rich in fiber and sugar, they help our bodies reach a healthy blood sugar level quickly after fasting all day. It's also recommended to break your fast with water.

This book includes my favorite recipes for Suhoor and Iftar. For those mornings when time is tight, try one of my 5-Minute Breakfasts, and for days when you fancy indulging in a more hearty meal for Suhoor, there is a selection of 20-Minute Breakfasts. For Iftar, you will find a wide variety of meals to suit you and your family—First Bites, Family Feasts, and Easy Meals, followed by Sweet Treats. The final chapter is all about drinks, from masala chai to bubble tea.

Take this book as your guide to nourishing, flavorful, simple, and Desified meals, perfect for the whole family to gather around and share for Ramadan, Eid, and beyond. Before you start, I would recommend taking a browse through the Desi Pantry section and stocking up on any essentials you may need.

SUHOOR

Wa bisawmi ghadinn nawaiytu min shahri Ramadan.

The translation of "Suhoor" in Arabic is "the last part of the night," referring to the fact that it is the meal eaten early in the morning during Ramadan, before the break of dawn.

The end of this meal marks the start of your fast, and it is followed by prayer. The time of this meal varies each year, depending on the month when Ramadan takes place. Within the month of Ramadan itself, the time of Suhoor also varies day by day as each daily fast gets longer or shorter, depending on what time the sun rises and sets and where you are in the world.

It's important to fuel your body with a hearty, balanced, and filling Suhoor meal. These first chapters include recipes for breakfast, which contain long-lasting carbohydrates, protein, and healthy fats to keep you fueled for as long as possible. During your Suhoor meal, make sure you are drinking plenty of water to keep yourself well hydrated.

Some tips for Suhoor to help ease your fast:

- Avoid caffeine, as it can cause dehydration. Try replacing your usual cup of tea/coffee with a decaf alternative, fresh juices, or milk.

- Eggs are full of protein and quick to prepare. Enjoy omelets and boiled or poached eggs with toast, naan, or paratha to make you feel full.

- Add a handful of nuts and seeds to your oatmeal or cereal for added protein and a healthy source of fat.

- Eat fresh fruit and vegetables for fiber, hydration, and nutrients.

- And of course, drink plenty of water.

IFTAR

Allahumma inni laka sumtu wa bika aamantu wa alayka tawakkaltu wa ala rizq-ika-aftartu.

Iftar is the meal eaten during Ramadan after the sun has gone down. It is often shared with large groups of friends and members of the extended family.

When breaking our fast at sunset each day, it's important that we hydrate well and ease ourselves into the meal after a day of abstaining from food and drink. Traditionally, Muslims break their fast with dates. High in sugar and fiber, they help our bodies quickly return to a healthy glucose level. The dates are usually followed by a refreshing drink and some nibbles before we sit down together for the main meal. The later chapters of this book cover recipes for those first bites, as well as for easy one-pot dinners, family feasts, and, of course, desserts.

Some tips for Iftar to help ease your fast:

- Always start your meal with something hydrating like a glass of water and a refreshing drink (find inspiration in my drinks section!)

- It's Sunnah (good habit) to break your fast with dates, as they give you a quick boost of energy after a long day of fasting.

- Don't stuff yourself! I know you're hungry, but now that your fast is open you can continue to gradually enjoy food into the night.

- Although it's tempting, try to avoid eating too much fried and highly salty food, as this just leads to thirst in the night.

DESI PANTRY

Achar (mango pickle) .... Sour and spicy preserved mango pickle; eaten alongside curries and breads.

Ajwain (carom seeds) .... Commonly used in Indian spice mixes.

Aloo bukhara .... Dried plums; used in Indian cooking.

Amchoor (mango powder) ...... Sour and tangy; adds a unique sweet flavor to grilled meats.

Atta .... Whole-grain wheat flour for making chapatis, rotis, and parathas.

Basil seeds (tukmaria) .... Similar to chia seeds; high in protein.

Chaat masala .... Spice blend used for flavoring masalas and (especially) snack foods.

Crispy chile oil .... Spicy oil containing crispy bits of chile, garlic, and other flavorings.

Curry leaves (fresh) .... Best when quickly fried in hot oil to release their flavor; good for adding to your turka (fried whole spice mix).

Fennel seeds (saunf) .... Similar in appearance to cumin seeds, but with a strong, earthy, aniseed flavor.

Ghee .... A type of clarified butter that is widely used in Indian cooking.

Gram flour (besan) .... Chickpea flour, used in pakoras and other deep-fried foods.

Kala namak .... Pungent black salt with sulphuric tones, from Northern India.

Kashmiri chile powder .... A mild, deep red chile powder.

Mango pulp .... Use canned mango pulp to make lassi (a mango-yogurt drink) when mangoes are not in season.

Methi (dried fenugreek) .... A bitter Indian herb used in Butter Chicken (page 114) and other curries.

Mustard seeds .... Packed with antioxidants and slightly bitter in flavor.

Papri .... Crisp pieces of fried wheat dough, used to make Papri Chaat (page 90).

Rooh Afza .... A concentrated syrup flavored with rose, which can be diluted in water or milk to make a refreshing drink, or used to flavor dishes.

Sev .... A fried chickpea noodle snack, often included in Bombay mixes.

Tamarind sauce (imli) .... A sweet and sour brown sauce made from the fruit pod of a tree.

Turkish green chiles .... Long mild green chile peppers, available in Middle Eastern grocery stores.

DESI
BASICS

CUCUMBER RAITA

Raita is a popular yogurt dip served with biryani, curries, and other South Asian dishes. Its cool and refreshing taste tones down the intense flavors of the food you are eating it with. (Pictured opposite, top right.)

MAKES ABOUT 1 LB 2 OZ (500 G)

1 cucumber

2¼ cups (500 g) thick plain yogurt

2 tomatoes, diced

1 red onion, finely diced

¼ teaspoon chile powder

salt and black pepper

Wash your cucumber and grate it into a bowl. Put the grated cucumber inside a clean tea towel and squeeze it to drain away most of the moisture, then put the cucumber into a large bowl with the yogurt.

Add the diced tomatoes and onion, sprinkle on the chile powder, season well with salt and black pepper, then mix to combine. Store the raita in the fridge until you're ready to serve it with your meal. It keeps for 2–3 days.

GREEN CHUTNEY

Chutneys are versatile and can be altered according to your taste and the meal you're serving them with. The base of this chutney is a concentrated zesty herbal paste, which can be eaten alongside curries, or stirred into plain yogurt for a lighter yogurt dip. (Pictured on page 17.)

MAKES 1 X 13 OZ (370 G) JAR

2 bunches of fresh cilantro

1 bunch of fresh mint

½ a white onion, roughly chopped

2 tomatoes, deseeded

2–4 green chiles

1 in (2½ cm) piece of ginger, peeled and roughly chopped

2 tablespoons oil

½ teaspoon sea salt

½ cup (120 g) plain yogurt, for serving (optional)

Carefully wash the cilantro and mint, then cut off and discard the bottom half of the stems, retaining the leafy part of the stems at the top of the bunches.

Put the cilantro, mint, onion, tomatoes, chiles, and ginger into a blender and blend to your desired texture, adding the oil and the salt as you blend. I prefer my chutney not to be completely smooth.

You can serve your chutney at this stage, as it is, or alternatively you can mix it into plain yogurt for a lighter yogurt-based chutney.

This will keep for 2–3 days stored in the fridge.

RED CHUTNEY

Red chutney is a sweet and spicy accompaniment to breads, snacks, and even breakfast. (Pictured on page 17.)

MAKES 1 X 13 OZ (370 G) JAR

2 large tomatoes, halved

1 small red onion, chopped

1 head of garlic, with the tops of the cloves cut open

4 dried red Kashmiri chiles

⅔ cup (60 g) unsweetened desiccated coconut

¼ cup (60 ml) tamarind sauce (imli)

1 teaspoon sea salt flakes, or to taste

Char your vegetables either in a hot oven or directly on your gas stove top, as follows.

Oven: preheat the oven to 475°F/240°C. On a lined baking sheet, lay out the tomatoes and onion. Wrap the garlic in foil, and place on the pan, then roast until the vegetables begin to char, between 15 and 20 minutes.

Stove: place the vegetables directly over a low flame (leave the onion whole if choosing this method, and wrap the garlic in foil). Rotate them regularly to prevent burning.

Put the charred veggies into a blender with the Kashmiri chiles, desiccated coconut, tamarind sauce, and sea salt flakes. Blend until smooth, then season with more sea salt to your taste.

Store in an airtight jar or container in the fridge for up to a week.

BASIC NAAN

This popular South Asian flatbread makes a soft and fluffy accompaniment to curries such as butter chicken, and is perfect for mopping up all that rich sauce at the end. Here's a super-quick and simple basic naan recipe that every Desi food lover needs.

MAKES 4–6

2 cups (260 g) self-rising flour, plus extra for dusting

2 teaspoons sugar

1 teaspoon sea salt

1 cup (230 g) whole-milk Greek yogurt

In a bowl, mix your dry ingredients: flour, sugar, and salt. Add the yogurt and mix to form a soft dough. Add a splash of water if the dough is too dry.

Tip the dough onto a lightly floured surface and knead for 5 minutes until smooth and stretchy. Put it into a bowl, cover with a tea towel, and let it rest for at least 1 hour.

Heat a tava or a heavy nonstick frying pan and preheat the broiler to medium-high. Divide the dough into 4–6 balls, depending on how big you want each naan, and roll them into oval/pear shapes about ¼ inch (½ cm) thick. Cook them one at a time in the frying pan over medium heat until beginning to bubble and puff up on one side.

Instead of flipping the naan, place the pan under the preheated broiler. It should take 4–6 minutes, depending on your broiler, but check after 2 minutes and keep an eye on it after that, until cooked through.

Repeat to cook all the naan.

PERFECT RICE

Many of the Iftar meals I share in this book are best served with steamed basmati rice. The formula for perfect fluffy rice is as follows: one part rice to two parts water, so 2 cups of rice needs 4 cups of water and so on.

SERVES 4

2 cups (400 g) basmati rice

4 cups (950 ml) cold water

Thoroughly wash your rice in cold water until the water runs clear.

Put your drained rice and cold water into a pot and bring to a boil. Gently stir, then cover with a lid and simmer over medium heat for 8 minutes.

Remove the lid, gently stir once more, then reduce the heat to low and cook for a further 5 minutes.

Turn off the heat, then fluff the rice with a fork and let it sit for 2 more minutes, to allow any extra moisture to evaporate. You'll be left with perfect pillowy basmati rice.

To reheat, place in the microwave with a splash of water and make sure it's piping hot, then allow to cool for a few minutes before serving.

YELLOW RICE

My simple yellow rice recipe is inspired by the rice served in Lebanese restaurants. I usually serve this alongside kebabs or grilled chicken, to jazz up a simple meal.

SERVES 4

2 cups (400 g) basmati rice

4 cups (950 ml) cold water

1 teaspoon turmeric

½ teaspoon paprika

1 vegetable bouillon cube

Thoroughly wash your rice in cold water until the water runs clear.

Put your drained rice and cold water into a pot and bring to a boil. Stir in the turmeric, paprika, and crumble in the bouillon cube.

Cover with a lid and simmer over medium heat for 8 minutes. Then remove the lid, gently stir once more, reduce the heat to low, and cook for a further 5 minutes.

Turn off the heat, then fluff the rice with a fork and let it sit for 2 more minutes, to allow any extra moisture to evaporate.

PERFECT ROTI

On many occasions in my childhood, I stood by my mother's side as she made rotis for the family. As she cooked each roti, it would puff up in the pan and she told me, "That means the person is extra hungry."

After many of my own failed roti attempts, I've discovered the key to making rotis that stay soft until the next day: use boiling water instead of warm or cold. The boiling water breaks down the wheat proteins, making the roti soft. Boiling water also partially cooks the flour, which allows the starch to absorb more water, and this produces more steam when cooking. Not only will your rotis be soft, but they will puff up during cooking.

MAKES 8–10

3 cups (400 g) atta (whole-grain wheat flour), plus extra for dusting

2 teaspoons salt

1¼ cups (300 ml) boiling water

Boil a kettle of water.

Measure the flour into a mixing bowl and add the salt. Measure and pour in your boiling water and at first mix well with a spoon, until the dough forms and it is cool enough to touch with your hands. Knead with your hands, using your knuckles to stretch the dough, then fold it over onto itself. Incorporate a splash more water if needed—this should be a soft dough. Knead for about 3–5 minutes, until the dough is smooth and crack free. Cover with a towel and rest for minimum of 20 minutes, until you're ready to cook it.

Divide the dough into 8–10 pieces, depending on how big you like your rotis to be. Roll the pieces of dough between your palms into smooth balls, then flatten them with your hands. Keep a bowl of atta nearby for dusting. Lay one of the dough balls on a clean floured surface and roll with a rolling pin to an ⅛ in (3 mm) thickness.

Heat up your tawa or heavy iron skillet on the stove until piping hot, then gently place your roti on it. After about 45 seconds you should start to see small bubbles appearing. Flip the roti over and cook for 10 seconds. Move the tawa away from the heat and place the roti directly on the flame—now it should puff up! As the rotis cook, wrap them in a clean tea towel and they should stay warm until it's time to eat. Repeat this process with every roti until your dough is used up.

TANDOORI SPICE BLEND

Tandoori spice mix is commonly used for grilling or roasting chicken, but it works wonders with fish, too! Apply it as a dry rub to your meat of choice, or stir 1 tablespoon of the spice blend into a scant ½ cup (100 g) of yogurt to create a paste for marinating.

MAKES 3¾ OZ (110 G)

2 tablespoons smoked paprika

2 tablespoons Kashmiri chile powder

1 tablespoon ground ginger

1 tablespoon ground coriander

½ tablespoon garlic powder

½ tablespoon ground cumin

1 teaspoon ground turmeric

Combine all the spices and store in an airtight container or jar in a cool dry place. You can prepare this spice mix in batches—it will keep for months.

CURRY POWDER BLEND

This is a simple spice mix that you can use to quickly Desify any curry, roast, or soup. Stir together the following few ingredients, then store in an airtight jar for months and use when you're craving a Desi kick.

MAKES 3¾ OZ (110 G)

2 tablespoons ground coriander

2 tablespoons ground cumin

1 tablespoon ground turmeric

½ tablespoon mustard powder

½ tablespoon ground ginger

½ tablespoon garlic powder

Combine all the spices and store in an airtight container or jar in a cool dry place. You can prepare this spice mix in big batches—it will keep for months.

SIMPLE MASALA

Many curries start with a similar masala made up of tomatoes, onion, and garlic. Masala, which literally means "mix," is a word that can be used to describe the saucy base of a curry. The spices and ingredients are altered depending on the type of curry you are making. This is a simple tomato masala recipe which can be used as the base or starting point of a lot of curries. Once your masala is made, simply add any veggies, meat, or fish of your choice. You could toss in some shrimp for a dry spicy curry, or add pieces of mutton and make a tender stew, cooked slowly over low heat.

MAKES ENOUGH MASALA FOR A CURRY TO SERVE 4

2 tablespoons ghee or neutral oil

1 large white onion, finely diced

5 garlic cloves, grated

2 tablespoons grated fresh ginger

1–3 teaspoons chile powder (depending on your preferred spice level)

2 teaspoons garam masala

1 teaspoon cumin seeds

1 teaspoon ground coriander

½ teaspoon ground turmeric

2 teaspoons salt, or to taste

1 tablespoon tomato paste

1 x 14 oz (400 g) can of chopped tomatoes

In a hot pan, melt the ghee or heat the oil. Add your onions and fry for 8 minutes, until they start to brown, stirring continuously.

Stir in the garlic and ginger and fry for a further 5 minutes, until the onions have completely caramelized and the mixture is fragrant.

Stir in the spices and salt and mix well. Add a splash of water if the paste becomes too thick. Cook for 2 minutes to remove the raw flavor of the spices.

Add the tomato paste and mix, again adding a splash of water if needed. The consistency should be that of a loose paste.

Stir in your chopped tomatoes and cook over medium heat for 10 minutes. Taste and season with salt to your liking.

SINDHI BIRYANI SPICE MIX

Sindhi biryani originates from Sind, Pakistan. It is spicy and notably zesty compared to other biryanis. Aloo bhukhara are whole dried plums—as they cook, the flesh of the plums melt away and the seeds are left behind. If you can't find them, you can use chopped prunes as an alternative.

MAKES 1 X 13 OZ (370 G) JAR

WHOLE SPICES

15–20 whole green cardamom pods

6 star anise

5 cinnamon sticks

5 mace blades

2 whole black cardamom pods

1 tablespoon cumin seeds

2 teaspoons black peppercorns

1 teaspoon cloves

1 whole nutmeg

OTHER INGREDIENTS

4 tablespoons Kashmiri chile powder

4 tablespoons ground coriander

3 tablespoons hot red chile powder

2 tablespoons ground cumin

1 tablespoons ground turmeric

1 tablespoon sugar

1–2 tablespoons salt

5–6 bay leaves

2¼ oz (60 g) aloo bhukhara (dried plums), or chopped prunes

Heat a frying pan over medium heat and add your whole spices to toast. Keep the heat low and gently warm the spices for up to 15 minutes, until they become fragrant. Remove from the pan and let them cool down before grinding.

It's important to let the toasted spices cool completely for a longer shelf life. You can grind the spices in the spice grinder attachment on your blender, a coffee grinder, or even a mortar and pestle. Grind to a fine powder.

Pour the ground whole spices into a jar or bowl. Then mix in the other ingredients and store in an airtight container for up to 6 months. Use as required. You can also freeze this and it should stay fresh for about a year.

BOMBAY BIRYANI SPICE MIX

Bombay biryani is a popular dish traditionally cooked with potatoes, but you can use this spice mix in other dishes too—for example, my Biryani-Spiced Chicken Bake on page 160.

MAKES 1 X 13 OZ (370 G) JAR

WHOLE SPICES

10 whole green cardamom pods

8 whole black cardamom pods

5 dried red chiles

2 cinnamon sticks

2 star anise

1 whole nutmeg

1 mace blade

1 tablespoon coriander seeds

½ tablespoon black peppercorns

½ tablespoon cumin seeds

½ tablespoon methi (dried fenugreek leaves)

OTHER INGREDIENTS

2 bay leaves

2 tablespoons chile powder

1 tablespoon ground turmeric

1 tablespoon salt

Heat a frying pan over medium heat and add your whole spices to toast. Keep the heat low and gently warm the spices for up to 15 minutes, until they become fragrant. Remove from the pan and let them cool down before grinding.

It's important to let your toasted spices cool completely for a longer shelf life. You can grind the spices in the spice grinder attachment on your blender, a coffee grinder, or even a mortar and pestle. Grind to a fine powder.

Pour the ground spices into a jar or bowl. Then mix in the other ingredients and store in an airtight container for up to 6 months. Use as required. You can also freeze this and it should stay fresh for about a year.

5-MINUTE
BREAKFASTS

MANGO BREAKFAST BOWL

These breakfast bowls are layered with creamy mango-infused overnight oats, fresh mango, crunchy granola, and fiber-packed basil seeds. Prepare the bowls the night before and store them in the fridge, ready for Suhoor.

SERVES 2

2 tablespoons basil seeds (tukmaria)

1½ cups (125 g) old fashioned oats

½ cup (125 ml) milk of your choice

½ cup (125 g) plain yogurt

3½ tablespoons mango purée

1 ripe mango, peeled, pitted, and diced

1 cup (100 g) granola of your choice

Put your basil seeds into a small bowl with 1 cup (250 ml) of water and leave to soak for 10 minutes until they expand.

In a large bowl, combine the oats with the milk, yogurt, and mango purée.

Layer each component in your serving bowls, starting with a layer of oats, then the fresh mango, drained basil seeds, and granola, and repeat until you have filled each bowl.

Cover and store in the fridge for up to 2 days.

ROSE OVERNIGHT OATS

This is a great recipe to scale up and prep in batches so that your breakfast is set for the next couple of days, making your Suhoor that much easier on a busy morning. Prepare this the night before and keep it in the fridge. Top with fresh fruit before serving.

SERVES 2

2 teaspoons basil seeds (tukmaria)

1⅔ cups (150 g) old fashioned oats

1 cup (250 ml) milk of your choice

1 cup (250 g) whole-milk Greek yogurt

2 tablespoons rose syrup, like Rooh Afza

TO SERVE

3 oz (85 g) fresh fruit
(I like strawberries)

¾ cup (85 g) granola of your choice

⅓ cup (40 g) mixed nuts and seeds

Put the basil seeds into a small bowl with 1 cup (250 ml) of water and leave to soak for a few minutes until they expand.

In a bowl, combine your oats with the milk, yogurt, drained basil seeds, and rose syrup. Store in bowls, containers, or jars and keep in the fridge until serving.

To serve, simply top with fresh fruit and granola of your choice. Finish with a sprinkle of mixed nuts and seeds.

NUTTY OVERNIGHT OATS

A quick high-protein breakfast that you can prepare in advance and store in the fridge. Top with granola or cereal and crushed nuts before serving.

SERVES 2

2 tablespoons crunchy peanut butter

1 tablespoon chocolate-hazelnut spread like Nutella

2¾ cups (250 g) old fashioned oats

1 cup (250 ml) milk of your choice

1 cup (250 g) whole-milk Greek yogurt

TO SERVE

2 bananas, chopped

⅓ cup (50 g) mixed nuts, crushed

½ cup (50 g) granola or cereal of your choice (optional)

Put the peanut butter and chocolate spread into a small bowl, then melt in the microwave in 10-second bursts, stirring between each, for up to 40 seconds or until softened.

In a bowl, combine the oats, milk, yogurt, and the melted peanut butter and chocolate mixture. Store in an airtight container or jar in the fridge until serving.

Serve with chopped bananas, a sprinkle of crushed mixed nuts, and granola or your choice of cereal.

SUPER BERRY OVERNIGHT OATS

This is a fruity refreshing overnight oats option, full of fiber and carbs to keep you fueled. Prepare this the night before and keep in the fridge until you need it. Top with fresh fruit and nuts before serving.

SERVES 2

2 teaspoons basil seeds (tukmaria)

2¾ cups (250 g) old fashioned oats

1 cup (250 ml) milk of your choice

1 cup (250 g) whole-milk strawberry yogurt

2 tablespoons goji berries

1 cup (150 g) mixture of blueberries, raspberries, and strawberries

½ cup (75 g) crushed mixed nuts or seeds

Put your basil seeds into a small bowl with 1 cup (250 ml) of water and leave to soak for a few minutes until they expand.

In a large bowl, combine the oats with the milk, yogurt, goji berries, and the drained basil seeds. Stir in half your fresh berries, then place in airtight containers or mason jars and store in the fridge until serving.

To serve, top with the rest of the fresh berries and a sprinkle of crushed mixed nuts or seeds.

BANANA DATE SMOOTHIE

Naturally sweet and rich in fiber, this smoothie can be whipped up in just a few minutes. Its long-lasting energy will keep you fueled for the day.

SERVES 2

2 ripe bananas, peeled

4 medjool dates, pitted

1⅔ cups (400 ml) oat milk, or milk of your choice

1 cup (80 g) old fashioned oats

1 tablespoon honey (optional)

Put all your ingredients except the honey into a blender and blend until smooth. Taste for sweetness and add honey if needed.

Serve chilled or over ice.

MANGO LASSI BOWL

You've heard of the "smoothie bowl" . . . well, here's my Desified take on this popular breakfast. Fruit alone is not a complete meal, especially during Ramadan, so this lassi bowl is topped with granola, nuts, and seeds, which are all packed full of healthy fats and protein.

　　You can prep this the night before—just top your bowl with cereal or granola before serving!

SERVES 2

2 tablespoons basil seeds (tukmaria)

2 ripe mangoes, peeled, pitted, and chopped

2 bananas, peeled

1 cup (240 g) whole-milk Greek yogurt

1 tablespoon honey

about 1 cup (200 g) ice

TOPPINGS

about 1 cup (190 g) blueberries

nuts and seeds of your choice (walnuts, almonds, pumpkin seeds, poppy seeds)

1⅔ cups (190 g) granola or cereal of your choice

Put your basil seeds into a bowl with 1 cup (250 ml) of water and leave to soak for a few minutes until they expand.

Put the mango, banana, yogurt, and honey into a blender with the ice and blend until just smooth (don't over-blend).

Divide your smoothie mixture between two bowls and top with the drained basil seeds, blueberries, nuts and seeds, and a big handful of your favorite granola or cereal (for crunch and carbs!).

MASALA BEANS ON TOAST

This spicy twist on the classic beans on toast is perfect for a lazy Suhoor or a quick brunch. Not only is it easy, but the beans are packed with fiber and plant-based protein for an excellent healthy 5-minute breakfast.

SERVES 2

1 tablespoon oil

1 red onion, diced

1 tablespoon tomato paste

½ teaspoon chile powder

¼ teaspoon ground turmeric

¼ teaspoon garam masala

1 x 14 oz (400 g) can of baked beans

salt and black pepper

crusty buttered bread or toast, to serve

Heat the oil in a nonstick pan, then add the diced onions and cook until brown. Stir in the tomato paste and a splash of water, followed by all the spices. Stir until it forms a fragrant paste.

Add the baked beans and gently warm over medium heat until piping hot. Once they start to bubble, reduce the heat and season with salt and pepper to taste.

Serve hot, on crusty buttered bread or toast.

DESIFIED TURKISH EGGS

All you need is 6 ingredients (plus naan and salt), 5 minutes, and the patience to poach some eggs. I'm not ashamed to admit that I'm terrible at poaching eggs . . . but if you're as bad as me, don't worry—I have an egg-poaching hack for you.

SERVES 2

1 cup (250 g) whole-milk Greek yogurt, at room temperature

2 garlic cloves, grated

4 eggs

3 tablespoons ghee

1 teaspoon garam masala

1 teaspoon chile powder

sea salt

a small handful of cilantro leaves (optional)

1 naan, toasted and sliced

Put the yogurt into a bowl and grate in the garlic cloves. Give it a stir and let it sit while you poach your eggs.

To poach them using the conventional method, bring a medium pot of water to a boil, then reduce the heat to a gentle simmer. Poach 1 egg at a time. Crack your egg into a small mug or bowl, stir the water in a clockwise direction, then carefully drop your egg into the center. Poach for 2 minutes for a runny yolk, or 3 minutes for a slightly firmer but still gooey yolk.

If (like me) you find the conventional method tricky, follow my hack below.

Grease a ladle by wiping it with an oiled piece of paper towel. Then place the ladle in a pot of boiling water, facing upwards. Crack your egg directly into the ladle. This is a foolproof way of poaching perfectly round eggs every time. After 2 minutes, simply lift the ladle and place the egg on paper towels to absorb the extra water.

Dollop some of your garlicky yogurt mixture onto plates and spread it out with the back of a spoon. Place your poached eggs on top.

Heat the ghee in a small frying pan. Once it's hot, add the garam masala and chile powder and let them sizzle for 1 minute.

Quickly but carefully pour the ghee over your eggs and yogurt.

Finish with a sprinkle of sea salt and cilantro to taste, and enjoy with toasted naan.

MASALA SCRAMBLED EGGS

Scramble your eggs into a tomato-based masala for a spicy, saucy twist on basic scrambled eggs. This is best served with parathas.

SERVES 2

1 red onion, diced

4 garlic cloves, grated

1 tablespoon oil or butter

5½ oz (150 g) tomatoes, diced

6 eggs

⅓ cup (75 ml) milk

1 teaspoon chile powder

¼ teaspoon ground turmeric

½ teaspoon garam masala

salt and black pepper

warm parathas or toast, to serve

In a nonstick frying pan, sauté the onions and garlic in the oil or butter until completely golden. Stir in the tomatoes and cook over medium heat until they start to break down into a sauce.

In a bowl, whisk together the eggs and milk until combined, then stir in the spices.

Pour the egg mixture into the tomatoes, stirring continuously. Cook for up to 8 minutes. As the eggs begin to set, reduce the heat and season with salt and pepper.

Serve with warm parathas or toast.

BREAKFAST GUACAMOLE

This is my go-to guacamole recipe. It makes for a filling, nutritious, and delicious accompaniment to your breakfast this Ramadan. Spread it on toast, spoon it into your breakfast tacos, or even save some to eat with tortilla chips for a late-night snack after Iftar.

You can prepare your avo mixture the night before and keep it in the fridge.

SERVES 4 AS A CONDIMENT

2 large ripe avocados, peeled and pitted

1 small red onion, finely diced

1 scallion, finely chopped

1 beefsteak tomato, diced

a handful of fresh cilantro, chopped

½ a red chile, very finely chopped

½ teaspoon paprika

½ a lime

salt and black pepper

Start by smashing your avocados in a bowl, using the back of a fork. Then stir in all your veggies, herbs, and spices. Squeeze in almost all the lime juice, season to taste, and mix well. Squeeze the rest of the lime juice over the top, then cover with plastic wrap and store in the fridge.

This will keep in the fridge for 2 days.

AVOCADO NAAN

Forget avocado toast . . . try this avocado naan! It's the perfect way to use up leftover naan from last night's dinner. Toast the naan until crispy, then top with spoonfuls of this lush avocado mixture.

The round Punjabi naans are usually bigger than the ones you buy in the supermarket, so you can use one Punjabi naan, or two regular naans.

Prepare your avo mixture the night before and keep it in the fridge.

SERVES 2

1 large or 2 small naan

4 heaped tablespoons Breakfast Guacamole (page 47)

a little butter

4 eggs

chile oil, to drizzle

Cut your naan into quarters and toast for a couple of minutes until warmed through and the edges start to crisp up.

Divide the pieces of naan between two plates, then dollop a generous amount of guacamole on top and spread it out with the back of a spoon.

Melt a little butter in a frying pan, and fry the eggs to your desired runniness. Place them on top of the avocado naan.

Serve and enjoy, with a drizzle of chile oil for some added heat.

MASALA OMELET

Masala omelet is a Desi-style omelet (and a popular Indian street food), flavored with the essential elements that make up a masala: garam masala, chile, and turmeric. Prepare this in just minutes and serve with parathas or a bread of your choice.

SERVES 2

2 tablespoons oil or butter

½ a white onion, finely diced

1 teaspoon Kashmiri chile powder

1 teaspoon garam masala

¼ teaspoon ground cumin

¼ teaspoon ground turmeric

2 tomatoes, diced

1 green chile, finely diced

6 eggs

a handful of fresh cilantro, chopped

salt and black pepper

parathas, naan, or toast, to serve

In a nonstick frying pan, heat 1 tablespoon of the oil or butter and sauté the onions until soft. Add the spices and cook for another 2 minutes, until fragrant. Transfer this mixture to a large bowl and add the tomatoes and chile.

Whisk in the eggs until well combined, then stir in the cilantro and season with salt and pepper.

Heat another tablespoon of oil or butter in the same nonstick pan, then reduce the heat and pour in your omelet mixture. Cover with a lid and cook for 4–5 minutes, until firm. Then flip and cook for a further minute.

Serve with parathas, naan, or toast.

DESI BREAKFAST SANDWICH

These 5-minute breakfast sandwiches are protein-rich, filling, and inspired by Indian street food vendors, who grill up Desi sandwiches lathered in green and red chutneys in just seconds.

SERVES 2

6 slices of halal turkey rashers

1 tablespoon butter

4 thick slices of crusty sourdough

2 eggs

2 tablespoons Green Chutney (page 18)

2 tablespoons Red Chutney (page 19)

1 large beefsteak tomato

½ a red onion, sliced

2 handfuls of arugula or baby spinach

1 ripe avocado, sliced or mashed

In a frying pan over medium heat, fry the turkey rashers for 2 minutes on each side until just crispy, then remove from the pan.

Add the butter to the pan, then add your slices of sourdough and toast them low and slow for 3–4 minutes on each side until warm and crispy. Remove from the pan.

Finally, fry 2 eggs, then remove them from the pan.

To assemble your sandwiches, add a dollop each of green and red chutney to two of the slices of sourdough. Layer each one with the turkey rashers, an egg, slices of tomato and red onion, arugula or spinach, and avocado. Top the sandwiches with the second sourdough slices, and enjoy!

20-MINUTE
BREAKFASTS

MASALA CHAI BRIOCHE FRENCH TOAST

If you like bread and butter pudding, you will love my masala chai brioche French toast. It's a one-pot breakfast bake, infused with a strong masala chai and served warm with dollops of fresh whipped cream. Prepare it the night before and simply bake in the oven for 15 minutes for Suhoor.

SERVES 4–6

1 cup (250 ml) Masala Chai (page 198)

6 eggs

1 teaspoon ground cinnamon

14 oz (400 g) brioche loaf, cut into 9 x ½ inch (1 cm) thick slices

1¼ cups (300 ml) heavy cream

1 tablespoon confectioners' sugar

⅔ cup (75 g) pistachios, chopped

Follow my masala chai recipe on page 198, then allow the chai to cool. Preheat the oven to 400°F/200°C.

Put the eggs, masala chai, and a dash of cinnamon into a large bowl and whisk until well combined.

Soak the brioche slices in the egg mixture for at least 10 seconds on each side, then layer them in a large baking dish.

Bake in the oven for 10 minutes, then increase the heat to 425°F/220°C and bake for 5 more minutes. The middle should be firm, and it should have a crispy golden top.

While it is cooking, whisk your heavy cream until stiff peaks form.

Take the dish out of the oven and allow it to cool for 5 minutes, then dust with confectioners' sugar and serve with dollops of whipped cream and a sprinkle of chopped pistachios.

SEVIYAN

Seviyan (pronounced se-vee-yah) is a sweet, fragrant, creamy vermicelli pudding that's traditionally eaten for breakfast but is sometimes also served as a dessert nowadays.

You can prep this the night before, and just top it with nuts, fruit, or granola before serving.

SERVES 4

2 tablespoons ghee

6 green cardamom pods

5½ oz (150 g) wheat vermicelli noodles

6⅓ cups (1½ liters) whole milk

2–4 tablespoons sugar

¼ cup (25 g) sliced almonds

¼ cup (25 g) chopped pistachios

Melt the ghee with the cardamom pods in a large pot over low heat for 2 minutes until fragrant. Crush the vermicelli between your hands, add to the pot, and toast for 4 minutes, until lightly golden brown.

Add the milk and bring to a boil, then turn the heat down to low and simmer for 10 minutes, until the vermicelli noodles are soft. Sweeten with 2–4 tablespoons of sugar, depending on your desired sweetness. Cook over medium heat until it reaches the thickness you like. I prefer it to be like a runny oatmeal.

Enjoy warm, with a sprinkle of sliced almonds and chopped pistachios on top. This will keep in the fridge for up to 3 days—to reheat it, just stir in a splash of milk.

KARAK CHAI FRENCH TOAST

Everything is better with chai, especially this French toast. My chai French toast is an indulgent breakfast, using ingredients you likely already have in your pantry! Brioche is a must to make it irresistible.

SERVES 6

2 eggs

3½ tablespoons Karak Chai (page 202), room temperature

14 oz (400 g) brioche loaf, cut into 6–8 x 1 inch (2½ cm) slices

1 tablespoon butter or oil

TO SERVE (OPTIONAL)

honey

strawberries or other berries

chocolate-hazelnut spread like Nutella

Crack the eggs into a dish and whisk. Add a ladle of your chai and whisk again until well mixed.

Gently poke each brioche slice with a fork, to allow the egg mixture to soak all the way through.

Heat the butter or oil in a frying pan. Dip each brioche slice into the egg mixture, let it soak for 30 seconds, then cook over medium heat for 4–6 minutes on each side until lightly golden brown.

Top with whatever you like. I go for a drizzle of honey, sliced berries, and sometimes chocolate spread.

CROISSANT FRENCH TOAST BAKE

You can use any croissants (or brioche rolls) that you may have lying around to make this simple one-pot French toast breakfast bake. You can prepare it the night before and put it in the oven in time for Suhoor.

SERVES 4

2 eggs

1 cup (250 ml) oat milk, or milk of your choice

2 teaspoons ground cinnamon

½ tablespoon sugar

2 tablespoons rose syrup like Rooh Afza

4 day-old croissants

2 tablespoons honey

a handful of fresh berries

Preheat your oven to 400°F/200°C (if cooking right away).

Use a baking dish that is just big enough to fit 4 sliced croissants. Crack in your eggs, add the milk, cinnamon, sugar, and 1 tablespoon of the rose syrup, and whisk until combined.

Slice your croissants horizontally (it's easier if they're a few days old) and soak them in the egg mixture for 30 seconds on each side.

Layer your croissants so they're just overlapping (see picture for reference). At this point you can cover your dish and put it into the fridge, ready to be cooked at Suhoor time.

Bake in the oven for 12 minutes. It should be just firm inside, with a golden crispy top.

While the bake is in the oven, make a glaze by combining the honey, the remaining tablespoon of rose syrup, and a splash of hot water to loosen. Allow the glaze to cool for a few moments before drizzling it on top of the bake.

Top with any fresh fruit of your choice—I like strawberries and raspberries.

CHAI PANCAKES

These chai pancakes are light, fluffy, and gently spiced. Serve them with your favorite toppings—I love clotted cream, cocoa, and honey or syrup.

MAKES 10–12

4 tablespoons (60 g) butter

2 cups (250 g) all-purpose flour

1 teaspoon baking powder

2 tablespoons sugar

½ teaspoon salt

1 large egg

1–1¼ cups (250–300 ml) Karak Chai (page 202), cooled

½ teaspoon ground cardamom

1 teaspoon ground cinnamon, plus extra for dusting

1 tablespoon ghee

TO SERVE

5½ oz (150 g) clotted cream or crème fraîche

1 tablespoon cocoa powder

honey or syrup of your choice

Melt the butter in the microwave, then allow to cool for a few minutes.

Sift the flour and baking powder into a large bowl and add the sugar and salt. Create a well in the middle, then crack in the egg and pour in the cooled melted butter. Mix well and gradually pour in the cold karak chai as you whisk. Add the ground cardamom and cinnamon, and mix until combined. Don't over-mix.

Heat a nonstick frying pan over medium heat and wipe a little ghee around it. Pour 3 or 4 tablespoons of batter per pancake into the pan and cook for 4 minutes on each side. The pancake is ready to flip once you see bubbles appear on the top. The underside should be golden brown. Repeat until you have used up all the batter, wiping the pan with ghee as needed. Stack the cooked pancakes as you go, and wrap them in a tea towel to keep them moist and warm.

Serve warm, topped with a dollop of clotted cream or crème fraîche. Finish with a sprinkle of cinnamon and cocoa powder and a drizzle of honey or syrup.

PUNJABI CHOLE MASALA

Chole masala is a popular breakfast dish of chickpeas that are quickly cooked in a thick tangy curry. Serve with Bhaturay (page 68) for a proper Punjabi breakfast experience—tear off a piece and use it to scoop up some chole.

SERVES 4

2 tablespoons ghee

3 cloves

2 green cardamom pods

2 black cardamom pods

2 bay leaves

1 teaspoon cumin seeds

2 red onions, finely diced

5 garlic cloves, grated

1 thumb-size piece of ginger, grated

3 tomatoes, diced

1 tablespoon garam masala

1 tablespoon ground coriander

2 teaspoons chile powder

1 teaspoon mango powder (amchoor)

½ teaspoon ground turmeric

2 x 14 oz (400 g) cans of chickpeas

a handful of fresh cilantro, to serve

½ a lemon

Heat the ghee in a large saucepan, then add the cloves, green and black cardamom pods, and bay leaves and fry for 2 minutes, until fragrant. Add the cumin seeds and red onions, and cook for up to 15 minutes, until the onion has completely changed color and turned a golden brown.

Push your onions to one side in the pan, then add the garlic and ginger and fry for 4 minutes, until the garlic starts to change color. Stir in the tomatoes and 1 cup (225 ml) of water, cover with a lid, then simmer over low heat for 15 minutes. The tomatoes should break down into a sauce, which will form the base of your curry. Add the ground spices and stir well.

Add 1 entire can of chickpeas (yes, including the liquid), along with another scant ½ cup (100 ml) of water. Cook for 10 minutes, until the chickpeas are soft, then roughly smash them down with the back of your wooden spoon. This will help thicken the sauce and will also give a variety of texture. Add your second can of chickpeas (again including the liquid) and cook for a further 10 minutes with the lid off, allowing any extra moisture to evaporate.

Finish with a generous sprinkle of cilantro and a squeeze of lemon.

BHATURAY

This simple fried flatbread is often eaten alongside Punjabi Chole Masala (see page 66), a tangy chickpea curry.

MAKES 8-10

4 cups (500 g) all-purpose flour, plus extra for dusting

1½ tablespoons semolina

1 teaspoon sugar

½ teaspoon salt

½ teaspoon baking powder

2 tablespoons vegetable oil, plus extra for shallow-frying

½ cup (100 g) whole-milk plain yogurt

scant ½ cup–¾ cup (100–180 ml) milk

In a large bowl, whisk together the flour, semolina, sugar, salt, and baking powder until combined. Stir in the 2 tablespoons of oil and mix again.

Now begin gently kneading the dough with your hands, while adding the yogurt. Slowly add a little milk at a time until you reach the desired soft dough consistency. Continue to knead with your hands for 10 minutes, or alternatively use a mixer for 4–5 minutes, until the dough is smooth. Drizzle a little oil over the top of the dough, then cover with a damp cloth and let it rest for 1 hour.

Once risen, tip the dough onto a clean floured surface and divide it into 8-10 equal pieces. Let them rest for up to 10 minutes while you heat enough oil in wide sauté pan or deep frying pan to shallow-fry the bhaturay. The oil is hot enough when a small piece of dough sizzles immediately when you add it to the oil.

Roll each piece of dough into a circle 1⁄16 inch (2 mm) thick. You need to roll them out very thin, otherwise they won't puff up properly. Gently place a bhaturay in the hot oil and slowly press down with a wooden spoon or ladle until it puffs up. Fry for 2 minutes on each side, until golden brown, then remove and drain on paper towels. Make the rest of the bhaturay the same way.

TANDOORI BREAKFAST POTATOES

These are diner-inspired breakfast potatoes with a Desi kick. They are best served with a crispy fried egg and a generous sprinkle of scallion greens.

SERVES 2

1 lb 2 oz (500 g) potatoes (2–3 large), diced

1 tablespoon salted butter

4 garlic cloves, sliced

1 tablespoon Tandoori Spice Blend (page 26)

1 teaspoon chaat masala, plus extra for sprinkling

2 scallions, green parts only, sliced

2 crispy fried eggs, for serving

Peel the potatoes and cut them into bite-size cubes. Cook them for 8–10 minutes in boiling water, until al dente—don't over-boil them.

Heat the butter in a nonstick frying pan, then add the garlic and fry for 5 minutes on a medium heat until just golden and crispy. Toss in your potatoes and fry until golden on all sides. Add the tandoori spice blend and a splash of water if the pan is dry, then turn the heat to high and fry until the potatoes are super crispy all over.

Remove from the heat and finish with the chaat masala.

Sprinkle with the scallion greens and serve with crispy fried eggs for brunch, or as a side for lunch, sprinkled with a little more chaat masala.

BREAKFAST CHAWAL

Think nasi goreng, but Indian instead of Indonesian. Fry up some veggies into a quick masala, then stir in cold rice left over from the night before—there's always leftover rice in the fridge! Serve with crispy fried eggs for a filling breakfast that's high in protein.

SERVES 2

2 tablespoons oil

1 scallion, chopped

½ a red pepper, diced

¼ teaspoon chile powder

¼ teaspoon garam masala

¼ teaspoon mustard seeds

2 tomatoes, diced

2¼ cups (400 g) cooked rice

2 tablespoons dark soy sauce, or to taste

2 large eggs

Heat 1 tablespoon of oil in a frying pan and sauté the scallion and red pepper until they just start to soften. Add the spices and allow to cook for 3 more minutes, until fragrant.

Add the diced tomatoes and a splash of water if the pan is dry, and cook until the tomatoes start to break down into a masala.

Add your cooked rice and mix everything together. Season with soy sauce to taste.

In a separate frying pan, heat the other tablespoon of oil until the pan is smoking hot and fry your eggs until crispy. The trick is to fry the eggs on medium-high heat for 3–4 minutes, so the bottoms of the eggs get crispy but the yolks stay runny!

Serve your crispy fried eggs on top of the warm rice.

ALOO PARATHA

This spicy potato-stuffed flatbread is cooked in minutes. It's one to prepare the night before, or you can make a large batch and keep them in the freezer, ready to warm up in just minutes for Suhoor.

MAKES 10

4½ cups (500 g) whole wheat flour, plus extra for dusting

½ teaspoon ajwain (carom seeds)

1 teaspoon oil

4 large potatoes

1 green chile, finely sliced

a handful of cilantro

½ teaspoon garam masala

½ teaspoon chile powder

½ teaspoon chaat masala

2 tablespoons ghee

salt and black pepper

Start by making your paratha dough. Put the flour, ajwain, oil, and ½ teaspoon of salt into a bowl, then add 1 cup (250 ml) of water and knead to form a dough. Rest this dough while you make the potato filling.

Cook your potatoes in boiling salted water until soft, then put them into a large bowl and mash. Add the green chiles and cilantro, all the spices, and another ½ teaspoon of salt, then mix together until smooth.

Divide your dough into about 10 equal-sized dough balls. Flatten them with your hands and place a scoop of filling in the middle. Then fold like a parcel to seal all the filling inside.

Make sure your surface is floured, then roll out each paratha to an ⅛ in (3 mm) thickness.

Heat up a tawa or a heavy-based frying pan. Melt 1 teaspoon of ghee in the pan before cooking each paratha. Gently place the paratha in the pan and cook over medium heat for a few minutes on each side, until cooked through and golden brown. Allow them to cool, then stack them on a plate to freeze or eat fresh!

To reheat, brush some ghee over each paratha and cook them in a tawa or frying pan for 3–4 minutes on each side, until they're piping hot all the way through and golden brown.

TOMATO & PYAAZ PARATHA

This flaky flatbread stuffed with tomatoes and red onions (pyaaz in Urdu) is one to prepare the night before. Alternatively you can make a large batch and keep them in the freezer, ready to warm up in minutes for Suhoor.

MAKES 10

4½ cups (500 g) whole wheat flour, plus extra for dusting

½ teaspoon ajwain (carom seeds)

1 teaspoon oil

4 beefsteak tomatoes

2 red onions, finely diced

1 green chile, finely chopped

a handful of fresh cilantro, chopped

2 tablespoons ghee

salt and black pepper

Start by making your paratha dough. Put the flour, ajwain, oil, and ½ teaspoon of salt into a bowl, then add 1 cup (225 ml) of water and knead to form a dough. Rest this dough while you make the vegetable filling.

Deseed and dice the tomatoes so the extra moisture doesn't make your parathas soggy. Put them into a bowl, mix in the red onions, green chile, and cilantro, and season well with salt and pepper.

Divide your dough into about 10 equal-sized balls. Flatten them with your hands and scatter over the veggies. Then fold each one like a parcel to seal all the filling inside.

Make sure your work surface is floured, then roll each paratha to a thickness of ⅛ inch (3 mm).

Heat up a tawa or a heavy-based frying pan. Melt 1 teaspoon of ghee in the pan before cooking each paratha. Gently place a paratha in the pan and cook over medium heat for a few minutes on each side, until cooked through and golden brown. Set aside to cool, and repeat with the rest of the parathas, stacking them on a plate to freeze or eat fresh.

To reheat, brush some ghee over each paratha and cook them in a tawa or frying pan for 3–4 minutes on each side, until they're piping hot all the way through and golden brown.

DESI SPANISH OMELET

This is a classic Spanish omelet with a punchy Desi twist. You can boil the potatoes the night before to save time, and cook the omelet fresh for Suhoor, or else prepare it completely the night before and enjoy it either cold or reheated.

SERVES 2

1 lb 2 oz (500 g) potatoes, sliced

2 tablespoons ghee

1 white onion, sliced

2 garlic cloves, sliced

1 teaspoon chile powder

1 teaspoon garam masala

½ teaspoon ground turmeric

1 tablespoon tomato paste

6 eggs

3 tablespoons fresh cilantro, chopped

salt and black pepper

Cook your potatoes in a pot of boiling salted water until just tender, then drain in a colander and set aside.

Heat 1 tablespoon of ghee in a large frying pan. Add the onions and garlic and cook for 3–4 minutes, until they are golden brown, then add the spices and tomato paste, with a splash of water if the pan is dry, and cook for 2 minutes, until fragrant. Gently stir in the potatoes and coat them in the masala, then set this aside to cool while you prepare the eggs.

Break your eggs into a separate bowl, season with salt and pepper, and whisk until well combined. Once your potato mixture has cooled, add it to the eggs along with the cilantro and gently mix to combine.

Set the frying pan back over medium heat with the remaining 1 tablespoon of ghee. Tip all the mixture back into the greased frying pan and cook over medium heat with the lid on until it's almost set. Gently flip it over (or slide it out onto a plate, then flip it back into the pan) and cook for another 3 minutes.

When the omelet is cooked through and both sides are lightly golden brown, slide it onto a plate and cut it in half to serve.

PROTEIN BREAKFAST BAGELS

Freezer breakfasts are a lifesaver during Ramadan. These breakfast sandwiches are packed with protein, veggies, and carbs to keep you fueled throughout the day.

MAKES 5

12 large eggs

3½ tablespoons milk

1 teaspoon paprika

½ teaspoon chile powder

1 red pepper, diced

2 scallions, sliced

2 cups (60 g) baby spinach, roughly chopped

½ cup (50 g) grated Cheddar

10 halal turkey rashers

5 bagels

butter, for spreading

salt and black pepper

Preheat the oven to 425°F/220°C. Grease two baking sheets, or line them with parchment paper.

In a large bowl whisk together the eggs, milk, and spices until well combined. Season with salt and pepper, then stir in your veggies and cheese. Pour the egg mixture onto the baking sheet and place in the oven for 8–10 minutes. The eggs should be firm throughout and lightly golden on top. Once cool, cut into squares.

Lay the turkey rashers and bagels on the other baking sheet and bake in the oven for 3 minutes, until crispy. Set the turkey rashers aside and slice the bagels. Spread the cut sides of the bagels with a little butter.

Now assemble your bagels with the squares of omelet and the turkey rashers. Repeat until you have 5 breakfast bagel sandwiches.

Enjoy freshly made, or refrigerate for up to 3 days. You can freeze them too, to reheat later for Suhoor. To freeze, cool, then wrap in foil. Place in the freezer. To reheat, defrost the bagels overnight, then open them up and place the halves face up on a baking sheet. Reheat in the oven at 425°F/220°C for 6–8 minutes until piping hot, then reassemble and serve.

BREAKFAST BURRITOS

You can prepare these Mexican-inspired breakfast burritos in bulk, then freeze them and reheat them in the oven or air fryer for Suhoor. Each burrito contains 1 veggie or chicken sausage and 2 eggs, making them packed full of protein for a nutritious and filling breakfast.

MAKES 6 BURRITOS

2 tablespoons oil

6 sausages of your choice, sliced

1 teaspoon paprika

1 red or yellow pepper, sliced

1 red chile, finely sliced

1 red onion, sliced

1 tablespoon butter

10 eggs

1 teaspoon chipotle paste

6 large flour tortillas

3 tablespoons pickled jalapeños (optional)

salt and black pepper

Heat the oil in a large frying pan. Fry the sausages for a couple of minutes, then take them out of the pan and slice them up. Put the slices back into the pan and sauté for 6 minutes, until they're cooked through and golden brown. Season with paprika, then add the sliced peppers, chile, and onion and fry for a further 4 minutes, or until they just start to soften. Don't overcook these—we want them to still have some bite, as the burritos will be reheated for Suhoor.

Melt the butter in a separate nonstick pan over low heat, then crack in the eggs, stirring continuously to scramble them. Season well with salt and pepper, and add the chipotle paste. Cook until almost completely firm. Again don't overcook the eggs, as they will cook all the way through when reheated.

Place a ladleful of each mixture in the center of each flour tortilla. Add the jalapeños, if using. Roll your burritos up tightly, then toast them in a warm pan for 3 minutes on each side until crispy and golden.

Enjoy your burritos freshly toasted, or freeze them if you like. To freeze, cool, then wrap in foil. Place in the freezer. To reheat, defrost overnight, then reheat in the oven at 425°F/220°C for 10 minutes, until piping hot. Alternatively you can place the defrosted burritos in the air fryer at 400°F/200°C for 12–15 minutes, until piping hot.

ONION BHAJI HASH BROWNS

If a breakfast hash brown and an onion bhaji had a baby, this is what it would be. Crispy patties of potato and onion, flavored with the essential spices that make the popular street food. Cook these in batches, store in the freezer, and reheat for Suhoor. They're delicious with eggs as part of a hearty breakfast.

SERVES 2–4

1 lb 2 oz (500 g) potatoes, grated

1 white onion, sliced

1 teaspoon grated fresh ginger

1 teaspoon chile powder

1 teaspoon garam masala

½ teaspoon chile flakes

½ teaspoon ground cumin

½ teaspoon cumin seeds

½ teaspoon ground turmeric

⅔ cup (60 g) gram flour (besan), plus extra if needed

1 egg

oil, for shallow-frying

salt

Red Chutney (page 19), to serve

Put the grated potatoes inside a clean tea towel and squeeze to remove as much liquid as possible. Put the potatoes and onions into a large bowl. Add the spices and the gram flour and mix well until combined.

Crack in the egg and continue to mix until you have a pakora batter. It should be thick and holding its shape, not runny. Add a further ½–⅔ cup (50–60 g) of gram flour if necessary. Season the batter with salt.

Heat the oil until it just starts to smoke, ready for shallow-frying.

Using your hands, form the mixture into 1 in (2½ cm) thick patties and gently place them in the oil. Over medium heat, fry each hash brown for 5–6 minutes on each side. Flip once they are golden brown.

To freeze for Suhoor, let them cool completely before freezing. You can cook them from frozen: reheat in the oven for 15 minutes at 425°F/220°C or in the air fryer for 6–10 minutes at 400°F/200°C (the time will vary depending on your air fryer).

Serve with red chutney.

FIRST
BITES

CHOCOLATE-COVERED
STUFFED DATES

Dates are traditionally eaten at Iftar, as their high levels of sugar, fiber, and minerals help the body's blood glucose levels to quickly return to normal after a long day of fasting. Prepare a batch of stuffed dates in advance to share with friends and family in the lead up to Ramadan.

MAKES 20

20 Medjool dates

⅓–½ cup (90–150 g) crunchy nut butter

9 oz (250 g) good quality dark chocolate

1 tablespoon butter

2 tablespoons milk

2 tablespoons crushed pistachios

2 tablespoons coconut flakes

Soak the dates in hot water for 10 minutes to soften them. Then cut a slit in each one and remove the pits. Open up the dates and lay them on a large plate, ready to stuff.

Fill each date with ¾ teaspoon of nut butter, then squeeze them shut and set aside.

In a microwave-safe bowl, microwave the dark chocolate, butter, and milk for 15 seconds at a time, stirring in between. This should take up to 2 minutes.

Dip the dates into the chocolate one at a time, using a toothpick to hold them. Make sure each date is fully coated, then sprinkle them with crushed pistachios and coconut flakes and lay on parchment paper to set.

Store the dates in the fridge until serving. They will keep well for up to 1 week.

BRIE-STUFFED,
TURKEY-WRAPPED DATES

Who says breaking your fast with dates has to be boring? These savory stuffed dates are salty, sweet, and smoky. Prepare lots in advance and share them with your neighbors!

MAKES 20

20 Medjool dates

3½ oz (100 g) Brie

½ cup (50 g) chopped walnuts

10 halal turkey rashers, cut in half

1 tablespoon honey

½ tablespoon chile flakes

Soak the dates in hot water for 10 minutes to soften them. Then cut a slit in each one and remove the pits. Open up the dates and lay them on a large plate, ready to stuff.

Stuff each date with enough Brie to almost fill it. Sprinkle with chopped walnuts, then take half a turkey rasher and wrap it tightly around each date. Repeat until you've used all the dates. If making these in advance, cover and put in the fridge for up to 24 hours.

Preheat the oven to 425°F/220°C.

Place the dates on a lined baking sheet. Drizzle with honey, sprinkle with chile flakes, and bake in the oven for 6 minutes.

The Brie should be melty inside, and the turkey rashers crispy. Let them cool for 5 minutes before serving.

PANKO-CRUSTED ALOO TIKKI

This is another South Asian street food classic. I've perked up this recipe with peas and a crispy panko coating. Not only does the panko hold the delicate spiced potato cakes together, but it adds a crunchy texture to contrast with the soft pillowy filling.

MAKES 8–10

1 lb 2 oz (500 g) potatoes (2–3 large)

1 tablespoon ghee

½ teaspoon garam masala

½ teaspoon chile powder

½ teaspoon chile flakes

½ dried mango powder (amchoor)

½ teaspoon sea salt, plus extra for cooking the potatoes

1 small red onion, finely diced

1 red chile, finely chopped

1 Turkish green chile, sliced (available at most Middle Eastern and South Asian grocery stores; not essential but deliciously crunchy)

¾ cup (100 g) frozen peas

2 cups (500 ml) neutral oil, for shallow-frying

2 eggs

4 cups (250 g) panko breadcrumbs, plus extra if needed

chutney, to serve

Peel and chop the potatoes, then cook them in a large pot of salted boiling water. Once completely soft, drain, then put them back into the warm pot to evaporate any extra moisture.

Add the ghee, spices, salt, red onion, and chiles, then mash the potatoes, ensuring you mix the spices through the mixture. It's okay if the potatoes aren't completely smooth—small pieces of potato add a nice texture!

Gently mix in the peas, then allow the mixture to cool until it's cold enough to handle.

Heat the oil in a shallow pan.

In a dish, whisk the eggs. Put the panko on a second plate. Take a palmful of potato mixture and roll it between your hands, then flatten it into a thick disc shape. Repeat with the rest of the mixture. You should have 8–10 patties.

Dip each tikki first into the egg, then straight onto the plate of panko. Make sure each tikki is completely coated in panko, then gently place in the hot pan.

Fry each tikki for 4–5 minutes over medium heat until golden brown on both sides, then place on paper towels to drain.

Serve with chutney (see pages 18–19).

PAPRI CHAAT

Think of papri chaat as Desi nachos. One of India's most popular street foods, papri are crispy chips of fried wheat dough, topped with spoonfuls of zesty chickpea salad, drizzled with sweet tamarind sauce, and finished with the Bombay mix of your choice (I like sev, the crunchy little noodles made with chickpea flour) and a dusting of chaat masala. Use my sneaky day-old naan hack to create a similar base to papri at home.

SERVES 4–6

1 day-old naan or 2 day-old pitas

vegetable oil, for shallow-frying

1 large potato, diced

1 x 14 oz (400 g) can of chickpeas

1 red onion, finely diced

½ a cucumber, finely diced

4 tablespoons pomegranate seeds, plus extra to serve

¼ teaspoon chile powder

1 tablespoon chaat masala, plus extra to finish

½ a lemon

1¾ oz (50 g) fresh mint, chopped

1¾ oz (50 g) fresh cilantro, chopped

⅔ cup (150 g) plain yogurt

2 tablespoons tamarind sauce (imli)

1⅔ cups (100 g) Bombay mix of your choice

salt and black pepper

Cut your naan or pita into 1 in (2½ cm) squares and shallow fry in hot oil for 4–5 minutes, until golden brown and completely crispy. Alternatively you can use store-bought papri.

Peel and dice the potato. Boil until just tender, then allow to cool. Drain and rinse the chickpeas and put them into a large bowl with the cooled potatoes, red onion, cucumber, and pomegranate seeds. Season with salt, pepper, chile powder, chaat masala, and a squeeze of lemon juice. Add half the fresh herbs, then mix well and set aside.

On a large serving plate, begin assembling the chaat. Start with a layer of papri or fried pita, then add the chickpea mixture. Dollop spoonfuls of yogurt all over, and add a generous drizzle of tamarind sauce, the Bombay mix, extra pomegranate seeds, and the rest of the fresh herbs. Finish with a big dusting of chaat masala.

CHILE CHEESE GARLIC NAAN

These puffy naans are topped with loads of garlic (you can never have too much garlic) and gooey mozzarella. A delicious way to mop up curry sauces and chutneys, or just as delicious to enjoy on their own!

MAKES 4–6

2 cups (250 g) self-rising flour, plus extra for dusting

2 teaspoons sugar

1 teaspoon sea salt

1 cup (225 g) plain Greek yogurt

4 tablespoons (50 g) ghee

½ teaspoon chile flakes

6 garlic cloves, grated

a handful of fresh cilantro, chopped

3½ oz (100 g) fresh mozzarella, sliced

1 cup (100 g) grated Cheddar

In a bowl, mix your dry ingredients: flour, sugar, and salt. Add the yogurt and mix to form a soft dough. Add a splash of water if the dough is too dry.

Tip the dough onto a lightly floured surface and knead for 5 minutes until smooth and stretchy. Put it into a bowl, cover with a tea towel, and let it rest for at least 1 hour.

In a small microwave-safe bowl, melt the ghee in the microwave in 15-second bursts, stirring between each, for up to 1 minute, then add the chile flakes, garlic, and half the cilantro, and mix well.

Heat up a tava or a heavy nonstick frying pan and set your broiler to medium-high. Divide the dough into 4–6 balls, depending on how big you want each naan, and roll them into oval shapes about ¼ inch (½ cm) thick. Cook them one at a time in the frying pan over medium heat until beginning to bubble and puff up on one side. Instead of flipping the naan, place the pan under the broiler. It should take 4–6 minutes, depending on your oven, but check after 2 minutes and keep an eye on it after that, until cooked through.

Brush a generous amount of garlic butter over each naan and sprinkle with the mozzarella and Cheddar. Put the naans under the broiler for another minute to melt the cheese, then serve warm.

MASALA CHIP BUTTY

This is a classic British chip butty (a french fry sandwich) with the ultimate Desi twist. These masala fries can be air-fried or deep-fried, and are then tossed in a savory hot sauce.

SERVES 4

1 lb 2 oz (500 g) potatoes (2–3 large)

vegetable oil, for deep-frying

6 garlic cloves, sliced

1 red onion, sliced

1 red pepper, sliced

1 teaspoon chile powder

1 teaspoon chile flakes

1 teaspoon garam masala

1 teaspoon ground turmeric

2 tablespoons ketchup

2 tablespoons any hot sauce

2 tablespoons soy sauce

4 brioche burger buns

1 tablespoon softened butter, for spreading

sliced scallions, to serve

Peel the potatoes and slice them into fat fries. Soak them in cold water for 20 minutes, then drain and pat dry.

Either air-fry—tossed with 1 tablespoon of oil—at 400°F/200°C for 35 minutes, or deep-fry them: Heat the oil in a deep pan over medium heat. It is hot enough when a small piece of bread sizzles immediately when you add it to the oil. Deep-fry the fries in batches and don't overfill the pan. Each batch should take 8–10 minutes.

However you choose to cook the fries, they should be fluffy inside and lightly golden on the outside. Drain on paper towels and set aside.

Heat 1 tablespoon of oil in a large frying pan and fry the garlic for 5 minutes until golden and crispy. Add the onion and red pepper and cook for 3 minutes, until just beginning to soften. Stir in the spices and cook for 2 minutes until fragrant, adding a splash of water if needed.

Add the ketchup, hot sauce, and soy sauce, and mix until combined. Toss in the fries and cook for 2 minutes, making sure each fry is well coated with sauce.

Slice your brioche buns and lightly toast them. Spread them with butter, pile a handful of masala fries onto the base of each bun, then close with the top half of the bun. Enjoy hot, with sliced scallions scattered over.

CHILE PANEER BAO

Bao buns are soft steamed Chinese buns that are often filled with meat, such as fried chicken or barbecue pork, or with shrimp. My Desi twist uses everyone's favorite, chile paneer.

MAKES 10–12

¼ oz (7 g) envelope active-dry yeast

1 tablespoon sugar

⅔ cup (150 ml) warm water

4 cups (500 g) all-purpose flour, plus extra for dusting

1 teaspoon salt

1 tablespoon oil, plus extra for brushing

½ cup (120 ml) warm milk

Chile Paneer (page 144)

Start by activating your yeast with the sugar in 3½ tablespoons of the warm water in a small bowl.

In a large bowl, mix together the flour and salt. Add the yeast mixture, oil, warm milk, and the remaining scant ½ cup (100 ml) of warm water, and combine. Knead on a lightly floured surface for 10–15 minutes, until smooth, then set aside and let the dough rise for 1–2 hours.

Divide the dough into 10–12 balls, and flatten them with your hands into ¼ inch (½ cm) thick ovals. Brush some oil over the surface, then gently fold each bun in half and place on a baking sheet for 1 more hour, to rise again.

Steam your buns over boiling water for 10 minutes, then let them cool for 1 minute before gently slicing and serving with a big spoonful of chile paneer inside.

FISH PAKORAS

These pieces of succulent white fish are marinated in ginger, garlic, and chile, then coated in gram flour and fried to crisp perfection.

MAKES 12–16

1 lb 2 oz (500 g) cod (or haddock or other firm white fish), cut into bite-size pieces

1 tablespoon grated garlic

½ tablespoon grated fresh ginger

2 teaspoons chile powder

1 teaspoon ground turmeric

1 teaspoon garam masala

1 teaspoon paprika

juice of ½ a lemon

salt and pepper

vegetable oil, for deep-frying

2¾ cups (250 g) gram flour (besan)

½ cup (125 ml) water

Green Chutney (page 18), to serve

Put the fish pieces into a large bowl with the garlic, ginger, chile powder, turmeric, garam masala, paprika, lemon juice, and a pinch of salt and pepper. Mix well, then leave to marinate in the fridge for one hour.

Heat the oil in a deep pot, ready for deep-frying. It is hot enough when a small piece of bread sizzles immediately when you add it to the oil.

Put the gram flour into a bowl and mix with enough water to form a thick batter that will coat the fish (you may not need it all). Dip the seasoned fish into the batter.

Take each piece of fish and gently place it in the hot oil, making sure you leave space between the pieces so they don't stick together when frying. Fry for 4–5 minutes over medium heat, until golden brown on all sides, turning them over occasionally so that they cook evenly.

Drain on paper towels, then serve with green chutney.

HALLOUMI PAKORAS

"Shall we get some halloumi for the table?" That's me. I'm an avid halloumi-sticks-for-the-table orderer. There's only one thing better than halloumi sticks and that's halloumi pakoras.

SERVES 4–6

2¾ cups (250 g) gram flour (besan), plus extra if needed

1 teaspoon chile powder

1 teaspoon chile flakes

1 teaspoon sea salt

½ teaspoon garam masala

¼ teaspoon ground turmeric

1 cup (225 ml) water

3 cups (100 g) baby spinach, roughly chopped

1 red onion, sliced

2 x 8 oz (225 g) packages of halloumi, sliced into ½ inch (1 cm) thick sticks

vegetable oil, for deep-frying

Green Chutney (page 18) and hot sauce, to serve

In a large bowl mix the gram flour with all the spices and the salt. Then whisk in the measured water to form a thick batter. Stir in the spinach and onion, then gently dip the halloumi sticks in, being careful not to snap them. Make sure the halloumi sticks are fully coated with the pakora batter.

If the pakora batter isn't sticking to the halloumi sticks, add 1 tablespoon more of gram flour to thicken it. Keep adding gram flour until the pakoras hold their shape.

Meanwhile, heat the oil in a deep pan, ready for deep-frying. It is hot enough when a small piece of bread sizzles immediately when you add it to the oil.

Deep-fry a few halloumi pakoras at a time—don't overcrowd the pan. Fry for 5–6 minutes, until golden brown and crispy on all sides, turning them over occasionally so that they cook evenly, then drain on paper towels.

Enjoy hot, with green chutney and your favorite hot sauce.

KEEMA SAMOSAS

If there's one food I associate with Ramadan it has to be keema samosas. These spicy meat-filled pastries are a freezer essential—prepare dozens in advance and freeze, then defrost and fry them to golden perfection for Iftar. To see how to fold your samosas, look at the photo overleaf.

MAKES 15–20

FOR THE DOUGH

4 cups (500 g) all-purpose flour, plus 1 tablespoon

1 teaspoon ajwain, (carom seeds)

½ teaspoon salt

1 tablespoon vegetable oil

1 cup (250 ml) water

vegetable oil, for frying

FOR THE MEAT FILLING

1 tablespoon vegetable oil

1 red onion, sliced

1 lb 10 oz (750 g) ground meat (mutton or beef)

5 oz (140 g) potatoes, peeled and diced

1 teaspoon chile powder

1 teaspoon garam masala

½ teaspoon cumin seeds

1 cup (150 g) frozen peas

salt and black pepper

TO SERVE

chutney (for homemade chutney, see pages 18–19)

Start by making the samosa dough. Mix the flour, ajwain seeds, and salt together, add the oil, then slowly add the water until the mixture forms a soft dough.

Now for the filling. In a large nonstick sauté pan, heat your oil and fry the onion for 5 minutes, until golden. Add the ground meat and cook until browned all over, then add the diced potatoes, cover the pan, and cook for 10 minutes over low heat. Once the potatoes are tender, add the spices and frozen peas. Season with salt and pepper.

In a small bowl, mix together 1 tablespoon of flour and 1 tablespoon of water to create your pastry glue. Roll out the dough and cut it into rectangles about 2 x 8 inches (5 x 20 cm). From the bottom of the rectangle, fold one corner up to meet the edge, then repeat again, to make a cone shape. Fill the cone with a heaped tablespoon of the meat mixture, and fold over twice more to enclose it. Seal tightly using the flour-and-water glue.

At this point you can either freeze the samosas, or deep-fry them for 4–5 minutes until golden brown.

To deep-fry, heat the oil in a deep pan. It is hot enough when a small piece of bread sizzles immediately when you add it to the oil. Deep-fry the samosas in small batches, turning them over occasionally so that they cook evenly, and don't overfill the pan.

Serve with a fresh chutney (see pages 18–19).

VEGETABLE SAMOSAS

These vegetable samosas are filled with a simple spicy potato mixture and make the perfect vegan appetizer. To see how to fold your samosas, look at the photo overleaf.

MAKES 15–20

FOR THE DOUGH

4 cups (500 g) all-purpose flour, plus 1 tablespoon

1 teaspoon ajwain seeds (carom)

½ teaspoon salt

1 tablespoon vegetable oil

1 cup (250 ml) water

vegetable oil, for frying

FOR THE POTATO FILLING

1 lb 2 oz (500 g) potatoes

1 teaspoon chile powder

1 teaspoon garam masala

½ teaspoon chile flakes

½ teaspoon ground cumin

¼ teaspoon ground turmeric

1 teaspoon sea salt

1 cup (150 g) frozen peas

TO SERVE

chutney (for homemade chutney, see page 18–19)

Start by making the samosa dough. Mix the flour, ajwain seeds, and salt together, add the oil, then slowly add the water until the mixture forms a soft dough.

Boil your potatoes until soft, then peel and mash together with the spices and salt. Stir in the peas and leave the mixture to cool.

In a small bowl mix together 1 tablespoon of flour and 1 tablespoon of water to create your pastry glue. Roll out the dough and cut it into rectangles about 2 x 8 inches (5 x 20 cm). From the bottom of the rectangle, fold one corner up to meet the edge, then repeat again, to make a cone shape. Fill the cone with a heaped tablespoon of the potato mixture, and fold over twice more to enclose it. Seal tightly using the flour-and-water glue.

At this point you can either freeze the samosas, or deep-fry them for 4–5 minutes until golden brown.

To deep-fry, heat the oil in a deep pan. It is hot enough when a small piece of bread sizzles immediately when you add it to the oil. Deep-fry the samosas in small batches, turning them over occasionally so that they cook evenly, and don't overfill the pan.

Serve with chutney (see pages 18–19).

OVEN-BAKED PIRI PIRI WINGS

Foolproof and flavorful oven-baked piri piri wings every time. I love serving these wings with yellow rice or fries, to really satisfy my takeout cravings. After receiving millions of views online, dozens of recreations, and positive feedback, it was a no-brainer that this recipe should be featured in the book. Serve the wings with Yellow Rice (page 22) or Masala Fries (page 95).

MAKES 12 WINGS

2 tablespoons tomato paste

1 tablespoon vegetable oil, plus extra for greasing

6 garlic cloves, grated

a handful of fresh cilantro, chopped

1 tablespoon smoked paprika

½ tablespoon chile flakes

1 teaspoon dried oregano

1 teaspoon sea salt

12 chicken wings, skin on

Preheat your oven to 425°F/220°C.

In a small bowl, mix together the tomato paste, oil, garlic, cilantro, paprika, chile flakes, oregano, and sea salt. Coat the wings with the paste, then place them on a greased baking sheet, leaving space between them to help them cook evenly.

Bake in the oven for 30 minutes, then increase the heat to 450°C/230°C and cook for a further 10 minutes, until the chicken skin is crispy and dark brown (almost burned) in places.

AIR-FRYER LOADED FRIES

Indulge in a less guilty version of loaded fries, topped with chipotle chicken, gooey cheese, chiles, and chipotle mayo.

SERVES 2–4

1 lb 10 oz (750 g) potatoes (3–5 large)

2 tablespoons vegetable oil

9 oz (250 g) boneless chicken, diced (or ground chicken)

6 garlic cloves, sliced

1½ tablespoons chipotle chile paste

salt and pepper

½ cup (125 g) mayonnaise

1¾ oz (50 g) dill pickles, diced

1 red pepper, diced

1 red onion, diced

scant 1 cup (100 g) grated Cheddar

2 tablespoons pickled jalapeños (optional)

2 scallions, sliced

1 red chile pepper, sliced

peri peri salt

Peel your potatoes and cut them into medium/thick fries. Rinse them with cold water until the water runs clear, then pat them dry with a towel. Drizzle with 1 tablespoon of oil and air-fry them at 400°F/200°C for 20–30 minutes, until cooked through and crispy (the time will vary depending on your air fryer). Alternatively, oven bake them at 425°F/220°C for 35–40 minutes.

In a lidded pan, heat another tablespoon of oil and brown your chicken on all sides, then add the garlic and fry for 5 minutes, until fragrant. Stir in 1 tablespoon of chipotle chile paste, season with salt and pepper, and cook with the lid on for 10 minutes.

Mix the mayonnaise in a bowl with the remaining chipotle chile paste and the finely diced pickles.

Load your fries with chicken, peppers, onions, cheese, and jalapeños (if you like), then bake for a further 5 minutes.

Finish with dollops of the sauce, a scattering of scallions and red chiles, and a sprinkle of peri peri salt.

DESI KOREAN FRIED CHICKEN

Cooked twice. Fried once in a tandoori spice rub, then tossed and simmered
in a sweet and spicy gochujang glaze.

SERVES 4

vegetable oil, for deep-frying

1 tablespoon Tandoori Spice Blend
(page 26)

1 teaspoon sea salt

2¼ cups (250 g) cornstarch

8 chicken drumsticks

2 eggs, lightly beaten

⅓ cup (75 ml) alcohol-free
gochujang

⅓ cup (75 ml) soy sauce

3 tablespoons ketchup

3 tablespoons brown sugar

1 teaspoon chile flakes

sesame seeds, to finish

Heat the oil in a deep pot until just smoking hot. It is hot enough
when a small piece of bread sizzles immediately when you add it to
the oil. Alternatively preheat an air fryer to 200°C.

In a bowl, mix the tandoori spice and sea salt with the cornstarch.

Pat the chicken drumsticks dry with paper towels, and dip them
first into the beaten egg, then into the cornstarch. Make sure the
drumsticks are fully coated, then carefully place half of them in
the hot oil. Fry for 12 minutes over medium heat, turning them over
occasionally so that they cook evenly, then increase the heat to high
and fry for a further 3 minutes for extra crispiness. Repeat for the
remaining chicken.

To air-fry, distribute the drumsticks in the air-fryer and bake for 30
minutes.

In a frying pan, heat the gochujang, soy sauce, ketchup, brown
sugar, and chile flakes until the sugar dissolves. Add a splash of
water if needed. Toss the chicken drumsticks into the sauce and
cook over high heat for just 2 minutes.

Serve hot, with a sprinkle of sesame seeds to finish. Enjoy as an
appetizer, or over rice for a main meal.

KOFTE

My mom's hack for juicy kofte every time is to add fresh tomato to the keema mixture. As the kofte cook, the tomatoes release their moisture, giving the kofte a juicy bite every time. The tomatoes also add a bit of sweetness, which I love as a contrast to the saltiness.

MAKES 12–15

3 tablespoons olive oil

2 red onions, finely diced

1 lb 10 oz (750 g) ground mutton or lamb

2 teaspoons chile powder

2 teaspoons smoked paprika

2 teaspoons garam masala

1 teaspoon chile flakes

1 teaspoon black pepper

2 teaspoons salt

2 tomatoes, finely diced

1½ cups (50 g) fresh mint leaves, chopped

1½ cups (50 g) fresh cilantro leaves, chopped

TO SERVE

Yellow Rice (page 22)

chile oil

sliced scallions or cilantro leaves

Heat 2 tablespoons of the oil in a large pan and fry the red onions for 10 minutes over medium heat until they are completely golden brown and caramelized. Cool slightly, then put them into a bowl with the ground meat, spices, salt, tomatoes, and herbs, and mix thoroughly until combined.

Form the mixture into 12–15 kofte (flattened meatballs). Heat the remaining tablespoon of the oil in a frying pan and cook the kofte, in batches if necessary, for 6–8 minutes on each side until cooked. You don't need too much oil, because as the kofte cook they will release their own fat and juices.

Serve the kofte on top of yellow rice, finished with a touch of chile oil and sprinkled with something green—scallions or cilantro leaves are my go-to.

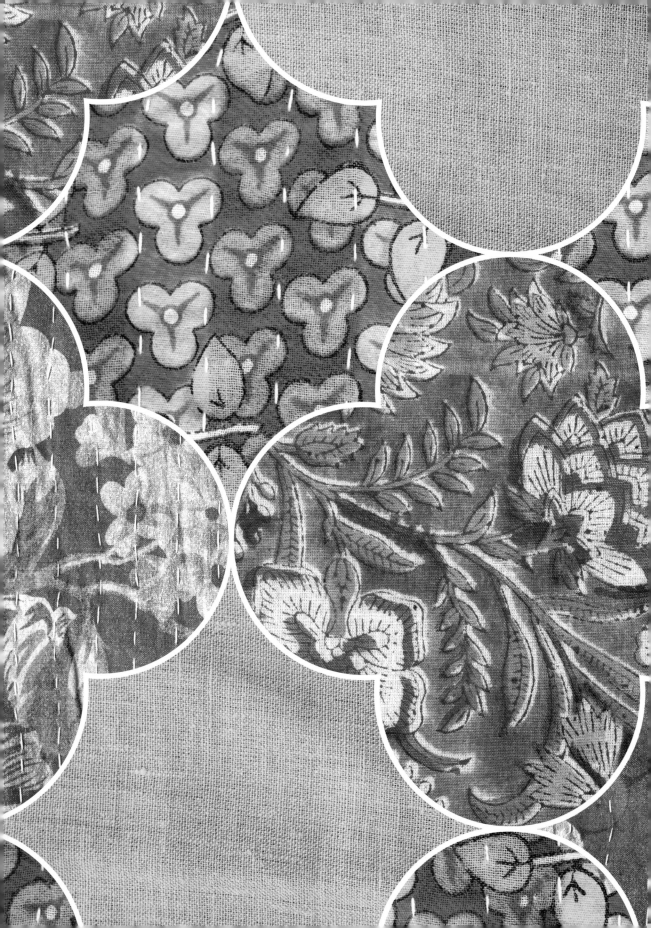

FAMILY
FEASTS

BUTTER CHICKEN

Aromatic pieces of grilled tandoori chicken are simmered in a creamy, spicy sauce. This is best served with warm naan, so you can mop up all that liquid gold sauce.

SERVES 4–6

1 cup (250 g) whole-milk plain yogurt

6–8 garlic cloves, grated

1 thumb-size piece of grated fresh ginger

2 tablespoons garam masala

1 tablespoon ground cumin

2 tablespoons chile powder

1 teaspoon sea salt, plus extra to taste

½ tablespoon ground turmeric

2 lb 4 oz (1 kg) boneless chicken, cubed

2–3 tablespoons ghee

1 onion, finely diced

1 star anise

1 cinnamon stick

4 black cloves

1 teaspoon cumin seeds

2 curry leaves

1 tablespoon tomato paste

1 x 14 oz (400 g) can of tomatoes

1 tablespoon methi (dried fenugreek leaves)

TO SERVE

⅓ cup (75 ml) heavy cream

a big handful of chopped cilantro

4–6 naans

Start by marinating your chicken. In a large bowl, mix the yogurt with the grated garlic and ginger and half of each of the spices—garam masala, ground cumin, chile powder, salt, and turmeric. Add the chicken pieces and mix with the marinade, making sure they're fully coated. Ideally let the chicken marinate in the fridge overnight, but 1 hour will be fine.

Now make the sauce. Melt 1 or 2 tablespoon of ghee in a large pot and fry the onions until golden and crispy. Add another tablespoon of ghee if needed, then add the star anise, cinnamon, cloves, cumin seeds, and curry leaves and fry for 2 minutes, until fragrant.

Add the tomato paste and a splash of water and mix into a paste, then cook for 3 minutes over medium heat, stirring regularly so it doesn't burn. Add the canned tomatoes, the rest of the ground spices and salt, and the methi, and simmer for 10 minutes over medium heat. If you like, you can use a handheld immersion blender to blend the curry sauce until smooth. Season with more sea salt to taste.

Place your pieces of chicken on a lined baking sheet or your grill— don't overcrowd them—and grill or broil for up to 12 minutes on each side. They should be cooked through. I prefer my chicken very well done and almost charred on the outside, for added barbecue flavor.

Add the grilled chicken to the sauce, stir well, then add most of the cream and most of the cilantro.

To serve, drizzle with more cream and an extra sprinkle of cilantro. Enjoy hot, with warm naan.

WHOLE PERI CHICKEN

This Portuguese-inspired feast is fun to cook and eat. It's versatile, so you can change it up with whatever side dishes you and your family enjoy, creating a big family feast inspired by a beloved chain of British chicken restaurants. Serve this with your favorite extras: salad, fries, peas, or corn on the cob.

SERVES 4

FOR THE CHICKEN

1 large whole chicken

1 tablespoon paprika

1 tablespoon chile powder

1 tablespoon brown sugar

½ tablespoon sea salt

½ tablespoon garlic powder

½ tablespoon black pepper

½ tablespoon dried oregano

1 tablespoon vegetable oil

3–4 tablespoons tomato paste

FOR THE RICE

1 red onion

1 red pepper

1 tablespoon vegetable oil

1 tablespoon paprika

1 teaspoon ground turmeric

½ teaspoon salt

1 teaspoon pepper

2 cups (400 g) basmati rice, washed (see page 22)

1 chicken bouillon cube

1 cup (150 g) frozen peas

Preheat the oven to 400°F/200°C.

Spatchcock your chicken (you can ask your butcher to do this for you, or look up the technique online: it's very easy). In a bowl, mix all the spices and oil into the tomato paste and coat the chicken with this paste, making sure every part is covered. Place the chicken in a roasting pan and put into the oven to roast for 35–45 minutes, depending on how big your chicken is.

Meanwhile, let's get started on the rice. Finely dice your onion and pepper, then sauté them in a large pot with the oil for 5 minutes, until soft and the onions start to brown.

Add the spices, salt, and pepper and fry for 2 minutes, until fragrant.

Add your rice and stir, then add 3½ cups (800 ml) of water and crumble in the bouillon cube. Bring to a boil, then cover the pot and let it simmer for 8 minutes over medium heat.

After 8 minutes, add the peas, stir carefully, then simmer for a further 8 minutes with no lid. Once the simmering time is up, turn the heat off and let it sit, allowing any excess moisture to evaporate.

Keep an eye on the chicken—once cooked the skin should be golden and crispy, and the inside should be white and juicy. If you squeeze the breast meat, the juice should run clear, which is how you know it's cooked.

Cut the chicken into quarters and serve over the rice, with fries and/or salad alongside.

TANDOORI CHICKEN & RICE

One-pot dishes like this one are life-savers on busy days, and just because you're cooking a meal in a hurry doesn't mean you need to sacrifice good flavor.

SERVES 4

8 chicken drumsticks

1 cup (250 g) whole-milk plain yogurt

1 tablespoon garlic paste

1 tablespoon ginger paste

1 tablespoon paprika

½ tablespoon garam masala

1 teaspoon salt

1 tablespoon vegetable oil

1 red pepper, diced

1 red onion, diced

1 teaspoon chile powder

1 teaspoon ground turmeric

1 teaspoon black pepper

1½ cups (300 g) basmati rice, washed (see page 22)

1 chicken bouillon cube

Put your chicken drumsticks into a large bowl and add the yogurt, garlic and ginger pastes, paprika, garam masala, and salt. Coat the chicken with the spicy mixture.

Heat the oil in a large, deep nonstick frying pan. Once the pan is hot, add your chicken drumsticks and cook them over medium heat for 15 minutes, rotating them occasionally.

Remove the drumsticks from the pan and set aside. Add the red pepper and onion to the pan and cook for 2 minutes, until they just start to soften, then add the remaining spices.

Give it all a stir, then add the rice and toast it in the dry masala for 2 minutes. Add 2½ cups (575 ml) of water and the crumbled bouillon cube, bring to a boil, then reduce the heat to medium and simmer gently for 8 minutes.

After 8 minutes, the rice should be half cooked. Place your chicken drumsticks on top of the rice, cover the pot with a lid, and cook for 10–12 minutes over low heat.

Remove the lid and finish cooking for 2 minutes, allowing any extra moisture to evaporate.

LAHORI CHARGA ROAST CHICKEN LEGS

Traditional Lahori charga uses a whole skinless chicken that is first scored deeply to allow the marinade to seep into the meat, then steamed until tender. After that, the whole aromatic chicken is deep-fried.

SERVES 4–6

6 chicken legs

1 cup (250 g) whole-milk plain yogurt

1 tablespoon paprika

1 tablespoon Kashmiri chile powder

½ tablespoon garam masala

½ tablespoon ground cumin

1 teaspoon ground turmeric

1 tablespoon grated garlic

1 tablespoon grated fresh ginger

1 tablespoon chaat masala, plus extra to finish

2 teaspoons sea salt

½ tablespoon black pepper

2–3 large red onions, halved

oil, for frying

½ a lemon

Score the chicken legs with deep horizontal cuts. In a large bowl, mix the yogurt with all the spices, salt, and pepper, then add the chicken and stir to coat. Put into the fridge and leave to marinate for a minimum of 2 hours.

Place the onion halves in the bottom of a large pot so they act as a stand for the chicken. Place the chicken legs on top of the onions and pour water into the bottom of the pot so it covers the onions but not the chicken. Cover the pot with a lid and cook over medium heat for 45 minutes, until the chicken is tender. Transfer the chicken to a plate.

Heat about ½ inch (1 cm) of oil in a frying pan. Put the chicken legs into the pan and fry over high heat for 2 minutes on each side, until crispy.

Serve hot, with a squeeze of lemon juice and a sprinkle of chaat masala.

KARAHI CHICKEN

Karahis are a type of dry curry unique to Pakistan. They are cooked quickly over high heat and use no onion—instead they are made with generous amounts of garlic and fresh ginger. Serve this with some warm naan or rice.

SERVES 2–4

4 tablespoons (50 g) ghee

1 lb 2 oz (500 g) boneless skinless chicken breast, cubed

6–8 garlic cloves, grated

4 thumb-size pieces of fresh ginger, grated, plus 2 thumb-size pieces sliced into thin matchsticks

1 lb 10 oz (750 g) fresh tomatoes, chopped

2 teaspoons salt

2 teaspoons chile powder

2 teaspoons garam masala

2 teaspoons ground coriander

1 teaspoon coarse black pepper

1 teaspoon chile flakes

1 teaspoon ground cumin

a handful of fresh cilantro, chopped

2 green finger chiles, sliced

naan or rice, to serve

Heat the ghee in a cast iron wok or other large, heavy pan. Add the chicken and sear for 4 minutes on each side, until it has browned all over.

Add the garlic and grated ginger and fry for 10 minutes, until they have completely browned.

Add the chopped tomatoes, salt, and spices. Keep stirring until all the chicken is coated in spices and the mixture becomes fragrant.

Keep cooking for 20 minutes—the tomatoes will break down and create a gravy. No water is needed, but feel free to add a splash if the mixture becomes too thick.

Finish with a big handful of chopped cilantro, the fresh ginger matchsticks, and sliced green chile, and serve with naan or rice.

CHICKEN BIRYANI

To make this dish, you start by cooking juicy pieces of chicken in a spicy marinade, then you layer the chicken between parboiled basmati rice and steam it to perfection. This is a fitting dish for an occasion such as Eid, or when you just feel like cooking up a feast.

SERVES 4

2 lb 4 oz (1 kg) boneless skinless chicken pieces, chopped

1 cup (250 g) whole-milk plain yogurt

½ tablespoon chile powder

½ tablespoon garam masala

2 teaspoons salt

2 tablespoons Sindhi Biryani Spice Mix (page 28)

3 tablespoons ghee

3 large red onions, sliced

6–8 garlic cloves, grated

2 inch (5 cm) piece grated fresh ginger

½ x 14 oz (400 g) can chopped tomatoes, or 12 oz (350 g) fresh tomatoes, chopped

2 cups (400 g) basmati rice, washed (see page 22)

a little vegetable oil, for frying

1 lemon, sliced, plus lemon juice to serve

a handful of fresh cilantro, chopped

Green Chutney (see page 18)

First, let's get our chicken marinating. Put it into a large bowl with the yogurt, chile powder, garam masala, salt, and Sindhi biryani spice mix. Keep this in the fridge to marinate while you fry the onions. You can also prepare it the night before.

Heat the ghee in a large pot and fry 2 of the onions until completely caramelized. This can take up to 15 minutes. Add the garlic and ginger and cook for 2 minutes until they become fragrant.

Add the chicken to the pot, allowing it to sear on all sides. Once it has browned, add the tomatoes and 2 cups (500 ml) of water, bring to a boil, then cover and cook for 10 minutes.

Parboil the rice for 6–8 minutes only. We're just going to half cook it, as it will finish steaming once we assemble the biryani.

Fry your remaining red onion in a little oil until crispy—about 15 minutes—and set aside until it's time to assemble the biryani.

Once your chicken is tender and fully cooked, remove the lid and let some of the liquid evaporate. You should be left with quite a thick gravy—it should not be runny, as you might expect for a curry, but more rich, like a thick masala.

In a large pot, begin layering your biryani. Let's aim for three layers. I start with rice as my first layer, because I love the crispy (almost burned) layer of rice you're left with at the bottom of the pot.

Keep layering rice, then chicken, until you've filled up the pot. Finish with a thin layer of rice, cover with lemon slices, then most of the fried onions. Then wrap the lid in a tea towel before you put it on the pot and steam over very low heat for 10 minutes. The cloth absorbs any extra moisture and leaves you with a fluffy biryani.

Serve with a splash of lemon juice, a sprinkle of chopped cilantro, and a big scattering of crispy fried red onions, with chutney on the side.

LAMB BIRYANI

We often cook a big pot of lamb biryani on special occasions, such as birthdays or Eid. You layer slow-cooked spicy lamb with parboiled rice, then finish the dish by steaming it. I like to make my own biryani mix, but store-bought biryani mixes can also work well.

SERVES 4–6

2 lb 4 oz (1 kg) lamb or mutton pieces (on the bone)

1 cup (250 g) whole-milk plain yogurt

2 tablespoons Sindhi or Bombay Biryani Spice Mix (pages 28–29, or use store-bought)

1 teaspoon chile powder

3 tablespoons vegetable oil, plus extra for the crispy onions

3 tablespoons ghee

3 large red onions, sliced

1 tablespoon grated garlic

1 tablespoon grated fresh ginger

1 x 400 g (14 oz) can of chopped tomatoes

2 cups (400 g) basmati rice, washed (see page 22)

1 lemon, sliced, plus lemon juice to serve

a handful of fresh cilantro, chopped

Green Chutney (see page 18), to serve

Put the meat into a large container and add the yogurt, biryani spice mix, and chile powder, then put it into the fridge to marinate for at least 1 hour, preferably overnight.

Heat the ghee and oil in a large pot and brown 2 of your sliced red onions until they're completely caramelized. This can take up to 15 minutes. Add the garlic and ginger and cook for 2 minutes, until they become fragrant.

Add the meat to the pot, allowing it to sear on all sides.

Once the meat has browned, add 2 cups (500 ml) of water and the tomatoes, bring to a boil, then cover and cook over medium heat for a minimum of 2 hours—the longer the better. I usually let mine cook for about 4 hours. Check on it every 30 minutes, giving it the occasional stir and topping up with more water if it dries out.

Parboil your rice in a generous 3 cups (750 ml) of water for 8 minutes only. We're just going to half cook it, as it will finish steaming once we assemble the biryani.

Fry your remaining red onion in a little oil until crispy—about 15 minutes—and set aside until it's time to assemble the biryani.

Once your meat is tender, remove the lid and let some of the liquid evaporate. You should be left with quite a thick gravy—it should not be runny, as you might expect for a curry, but rich, like a thick masala.

In a large pot, begin layering your biryani. I aim for three or four layers, starting with rice as my first layer because I love the crispy (almost burned) layer you're left with at the bottom of the pot.

Keep layering rice, then meat, until you've filled up the pot. Finish with a thin layer of rice, cover with lemon slices, the crispy fried onion (set aside a tablespoon to garnish), and a handful of chopped cilantro, then wrap the lid in a tea towel and steam over very low heat for 20 minutes. The cloth absorbs any extra moisture and leaves you with a fluffy biryani.

Serve with a splash of lemon juice, a sprinkle of chopped cilantro, and a big scattering of crispy fried red onions, with chutney on the side.

ALOO KEEMA

A true comfort meal of succulent ground meat that's simmered in a tomato-based curry before potatoes are added. Serve this with rotis (my preferred option) or rice.

SERVES 4

2 tablespoons ghee

6 garlic cloves, grated

1 thumb-size piece of ginger, sliced into matchsticks

1 red onion, sliced

2 bay leaves

2 teaspoons chile powder

1 teaspoon garam masala

1 teaspoon ground coriander

½ teaspoon mustard seeds

1 teaspoon black pepper

½ teaspoon sea salt

1 lb 10 oz (750 g) ground mutton (or beef or lamb)

1 x 14 oz (400 g) can of chopped tomatoes

3 large potatoes, peeled and chopped

a handful of fresh cilantro, chopped

rotis or rice, to serve

Heat the ghee over medium heat in a large pot. Add the garlic, ginger, and red onion and fry until the onion has completely caramelized. This can take up to 10 minutes.

Add the bay leaves, followed by the rest of the spices and the salt, and fry for 2 minutes, until they become fragrant.

Add the ground meat and keep stirring until it has browned all over.

Add the tomatoes, stir gently, then cover with a lid and allow to simmer for 30–40 minutes. Stir regularly to make sure there's no sticking. Add a splash of water if the mixture dries up.

After 40 minutes, stir in the potatoes cover once more, and cook for a further 30 minutes.

Finish with a big handful of chopped cilantro and serve with rotis or rice.

OVEN-ROASTED
LAHORI MUTTON CHOPS

This dish of slow-cooked mutton chops in a Lahori-style marinade is inspired by the flavors of Lahore street food. Finish the tender chops off in a grill pan to emulate the char of a tandoori oven.

SERVES 4

1 tablespoon methi
(dried fenugreek leaves)

1½ cups (350 g) whole-milk
plain yogurt

2 tablespoons good quality olive oil

6–8 garlic cloves, grated

2 teaspoons chile powder

2 teaspoons garam masala

1 teaspoon paprika

1 teaspoon cumin seeds

1 teaspoon sea salt

a handful of fresh mint, chopped

2 lb 4 oz (1 kg) mutton chops

Soak the methi in a small bowl of warm water for 10 minutes until soft, then drain.

In a large bowl, mix the yogurt with the olive oil, garlic, spices, salt, and mint, then stir in the drained methi. Add the mutton chops and stir to coat in the marinade, then put into the fridge for a minimum of 2 hours before cooking.

Preheat the oven to 400°F/200°C. Put the mutton chops into a deep baking dish, cover with foil, and roast for a minimum of 2 hours, until completely tender. Alternatively, pressure cook for 30 minutes.

Finish the chops by searing for 1 minute on each side in a sizzling hot grill pan.

Serve with naan, salad, and chutney (see pages 18–19).

KARAHI GOSHT

Karahi gosht is a famous Lahori dish of tender lamb pieces cooked in a thick, spicy gravy. It's a popular street food, cooked in large tavas in Lahore food markets, but easy to replicate at home in a heavy wok.

SERVES 2–4

2 tablespoons ghee

1 lb 2 oz (500 g) boneless lamb or mutton pieces

6–8 garlic cloves, sliced

2 tablespoons sliced fresh ginger

4–6 tomatoes, chopped

SPICES

2 teaspoons chile powder

1 teaspoon paprika

1 teaspoon ground cumin

1 teaspoon chile flakes

1 teaspoon cumin seeds

1 teaspoon salt

½ teaspoon ground coriander

½ teaspoon garam masala

½ teaspoon black pepper

TO SERVE

a big handful of fresh cilantro, chopped

2 green chiles, sliced (optional)

Heat the ghee in a cast iron wok or other deep, heavy pan. Add the meat and sear on all sides, making sure it has browned all over.

Add the garlic and ginger and fry for 5 minutes, until the garlic is just starting to brown. Then add all the spices and fry for a further 3 minutes, stirring constantly until all the meat is coated in the spices and the mixture becomes fragrant.

Pour in about 2 cups (500 ml) of water, or enough to cover the meat, bring to a boil, then turn the heat down to low, cover the pan, and allow to simmer for 2–3 hours, until the meat is tender. Make sure you check the pan every 30 minutes and top it up with a splash more water if needed.

Once the meat is tender, add the chopped tomatoes and turn the heat to high. Keep mixing, scraping the bottom of the pan as you mix to get all that flavor. The tomatoes will break down and, as the karahi thickens, it will create a flavorful, thick masala.

Finish with a big handful of chopped cilantro and a few fresh chile slices if you like it spicy!

CHEATER'S "BIRRIA" TACOS

If you've spent any time browsing for food inspo online, you'll have seen the viral birria tacos that are all over social media. This is not an authentic birria taco recipe, it's an accessible way of making some meaty, juicy tacos with ingredients you can find at your local supermarket, without having to track down specific types of imported dried chiles.

SERVES 4

2 lb 4 oz (1 kg) beef chuck or top sirloin (or boneless lamb)

salt and black pepper

1 large onion, chopped

½ a habanero chile

1 bird's-eye chile

6 whole cloves

2 bay leaves

1 cinnamon stick

2 tablespoons chipotle chile paste

4¼ cups (1 liter) water

2 beefsteak tomatoes

1 red onion

a handful of fresh cilantro

1 jalapeño

2 limes (1 sliced for serving)

sea salt

8–10 corn tortillas

9 oz (250 g) firm mozzarella, grated

Generously season the meat with salt and black pepper, then sear in a large pot for up to 15–20 minutes.

Add the onion, habanero and bird's-eye chiles (don't slice or chop the chiles—leave them whole), and the cloves, bay leaves and cinnamon, and fry for 3 minutes, until fragrant.

Add the chipotle chile paste and enough water to cover the lamb. Bring to a boil, then cover the pot and cook over medium heat for a minimum of 3 hours. Check it every 30 minutes, stirring occasionally, and top up with more water if needed. The longer you slow-cook this, the better the end result! I recommend 5 hours.

Meanwhile, prepare the fresh tomato salsa. Dice your tomatoes and red onion and place in a bowl. Finely chop the cilantro and jalapeño, and add to the bowl with a big squeeze of lime juice. Season with sea salt and set aside.

After 3 hours, remove the beef from the pot and shred it. Keep the sauce at a simmer and allow it to thicken for 10 minutes.

Heat up a skillet or frying pan. Dip each tortilla into the pot of sauce, then fill it with shredded beef, a spoonful of the sauce, and a sprinkle of grated mozzarella. Fold in half, then place in the hot pan and cook for 3 minutes on each side until golden brown. Repeat until you have filled and cooked all the tortillas.

Serve with lime slices, the fresh salsa, and a small bowl of the sauce for dipping.

NIHARI

SERVES 4–6

2 lb 4 oz (1 kg) mutton shanks (or lamb shanks)

2 tablespoons ghee

1 tablespoon ginger paste

1 tablespoon garlic paste

4 large onions, sliced

scant ½ cup (50 g) flour

NIHARI SPICE MIX

1 tablespoon saunf (fennel seeds)

1 tablespoon cumin seeds

1 tablespoon coriander seeds or ground coriander

1 teaspoon black peppercorns

1 cinnamon stick

2 black cardamom pods

5 green cardamom pods

7 cloves

2 bay leaves

2 teaspoons chile powder

1 teaspoon garam masala

½ teaspoon ground turmeric

1 teaspoon sea salt

TO SERVE

½ a bunch of fresh cilantro, chopped

2 thumb-size pieces of fresh ginger, cut into matchsticks

2 lemons, cut into quarters

4–6 naans

A popular Pakistani curry, in which slow-cooked meat is topped with handfuls of crispy fried onions. Fried onions are a vital part of nihari, as they help create the uniquely rich flavor of this dish. Nihari is traditionally made with beef, but my recipe uses mutton shanks (a more affordable alternative to lamb shanks).

To make the spice mix, grind all the whole spices to a fine powder, then stir in the chile powder, garam masala, turmeric, and salt.

Heat a large pot (or a pressure cooker), and sear the mutton shanks in the ghee on all sides until brown. Add the ginger, garlic, and 2 sliced onions and cook for up to 15 minutes, until completely caramelized and crispy. Stir in the spice mix and cook for a further 2 minutes, until the spices become fragrant, then pour in enough water to cover the meat (around 4¼ cups/1 liter). Simmer with the lid on for a minimum of 3 hours (or pressure cook for 45 minutes), until the meat is fall-off-the-bone tender.

Meanwhile, in a separate pan, shallow fry the 2 remaining onions until brown and crispy, and set aside.

Mix the flour with 1–2 tablespoons of water in a small bowl to make a slurry to thicken the gravy. Make sure there are no lumps, then slowly stir it into the nihari and simmer over high heat for 10 minutes, to get it to your desired thickness. Serve with the cilantro and ginger sprinkled on top, the lemon quarters and naan bread alongside, and lots of crispy fried onions scattered over.

SLOW-COOKED LAMB STEAKS

While I almost always reach for a fatty rib-eye when cooking a steak dinner, I wanted to share a leaner, non-beef option with you. These lamb steaks are slow-cooked until tender, then sear them in a soy glaze for a sweet and salty finish.

SERVES 2

2 bone-in lamb leg steaks (about 10 oz/280 g each)

1 lb 2 oz (500 g) baby potatoes

1 tablespoon harissa paste

2 teaspoons sea salt

1 teaspoon chile flakes

2 tablespoons honey

1 tablespoon ghee

6 garlic cloves, sliced

2 tablespoons soy sauce

1 red chile, sliced

Preheat the oven to 425°F/220°C and line a baking sheet with parchment paper.

First, either cook your lamb steaks in a pressure cooker for 30 minutes, or put them into a sauté pan, cover with water, and boil for 2 hours, checking occasionally and topping up with water when needed. While the lamb tenderizes, prepare the potatoes.

Boil the potatoes for 10–12 minutes (depending on size), until tender, then drain and toss them with the harissa, sea salt, and chile flakes. Lay them in a baking sheet, drizzle with 1 tablespoon of honey, and roast in the oven for 30 minutes. Check occasionally and rotate the potatoes for even cooking.

Once the steaks are tender, melt the ghee in a cast iron or other heavy grill pan. Fry the garlic until golden and crisp, then add the soy sauce, red chile, the remaining 1 tablespoon of honey, and a splash of water if needed. Add your lamb steaks and cook in the glaze for 2 minutes on each side.

Plate up with the potatoes, and don't forget to add the crispy garlic mixture on top (that's my favorite part!).

KABULI LAMB PILAU

Lamb pilau is a fragrant dish found in both South Asia and the Middle East. This is my version, which combines the techniques from traditional Kabuli and Pakistani recipes. It's topped with caramelized slices of carrot, the sweetness of which complement the savory rice.

SERVES 4

⅔ cup (100 g) pine nuts

4 tablespoons ghee

2 white onions, sliced

6–8 green cardamom pods

5 black cloves

2 bay leaves

1 cinnamon stick

1 star anise

2 teaspoons cumin seeds

1 teaspoon ground cumin

1 teaspoon salt

1 teaspoon black pepper

2 lb 4 oz (1 kg) lamb neck (or mutton)

2 cups (400 g) basmati rice, washed (see page 22)

3½ tablespoons (50 g) butter

2 large carrots, cut into thin matchsticks

⅔ cup (100 g) raisins

1 tablespoon honey (or sugar)

In a large heavy pot or pressure cooker, start by frying the pine nuts in 2 tablespoons of the ghee for 2 minutes over medium heat until they're golden brown.

Remove the pine nuts from the pot and set aside. Add the onions and fry for up to 15 minutes, until they completely change color to a dark brown (not burned, just very crispy).

Add your spices, salt, and pepper and fry for a further 2 minutes, until fragrant.

Add the lamb neck pieces and cook for 5 minutes on each side, until they've browned evenly. Add about 2 cups (500 ml) of water, or enough to cover the meat, then simmer over medium heat for a minimum of 2 hours, until the lamb is fall-off-the-bone tender. Keep topping up with water as needed. Alternatively pressure cook for 45 minutes.

Once the lamb is tender, there should be about 1 cup (250 ml) of liquid left in the pot. Add the rice and 2 cups (500 ml) of water, bring to a boil, then cover the pot and boil over medium heat for 10 minutes. Remove the lid for the last 4–5 minutes to allow any extra moisture to evaporate.

Melt the butter in a frying pan and sauté the carrots for 5 minutes. Add the raisins and honey, and cook for a further 2 minutes on high heat until sticky and caramelized. The carrots should be just tender, not mushy.

Serve the pilau and garnish with the pine nuts and carrots.

DESI DETROIT-STYLE PIZZA

Detroit-style pizza is authentically made in a rectangular baking sheet, with cheese sprinkled around the border to form its iconic crust and three strips of pizza sauce poured across the top. For a Desi twist we'll be making a spicy turka pizza sauce—turka is the process of quickly frying whole spices and herbs to release their flavor.

SERVES 6–8

FOR THE BEST DOUGH EVER

4 cups (500 g) strong bread flour

¼ oz (7 g) envelope of instant yeast

1 tablespoon sugar

1 teaspoon baking powder

1 teaspoon salt

1 cup (250 ml) hot milk

2 tablespoons neutral oil

FOR THE PIZZA

2 tablespoons olive oil

6 garlic cloves, sliced

a handful of curry leaves
(12–15 leaves)

1 teaspoon chile flakes

2¼ cups (500 g) passata or
tomato sauce

sea salt

1¾ cups (200 g) grated mozzarella

1¾ cups (200 g) grated Cheddar

12–15 slices of halal pepperoni

pickled jalapeños

Start by making your pizza dough. In a large bowl, mix together 1⅔ cups (200 g) of the flour, the yeast, sugar, baking powder, salt, and hot milk until it forms a thick batter. Let this sit for 20 minutes while it activates. Add the neutral oil and the remaining flour, knead for 10 minutes until you have a smooth dough, then put it back into the bowl and cover with plastic wrap. Let it rise in a warm place for at least 1 hour.

Preheat your oven to 400°F/200°C. Once the dough has risen, stretch it out to line the base of a 9 x 13 x 2 inch (23 x 33 x 5 cm) baking dish and let it rest for 30 minutes. Flatten the dough out in the dish with your hands once more, then bake for the pizza base for 10 minutes, until it's half cooked.

Turn the oven up to 425°F/220°C.

Heat the olive oil in a medium sized sauté pan until smoking hot, and fry the garlic over high heat for 2 minutes, until lightly golden. Add the curry leaves and quickly fry for up to 30 seconds, just enough time to wilt them and release their flavor. Reduce the heat to low, then stir in the chile flakes, passata, and sea salt to taste and simmer for 5 minutes to thicken.

Assemble the pizza: distribute the grated mozzarella around the border of the pizza (as the pizza cooks, the mozzarella will melt down the sides and create the crispy border). Sprinkle the Cheddar across the top. Spoon 3 stripes of sauce lengthways across the top of the pizza and finish it with pepperoni and as many jalapeños as you can handle!

Bake in the oven for 20–25 minutes, to cheesy perfection.

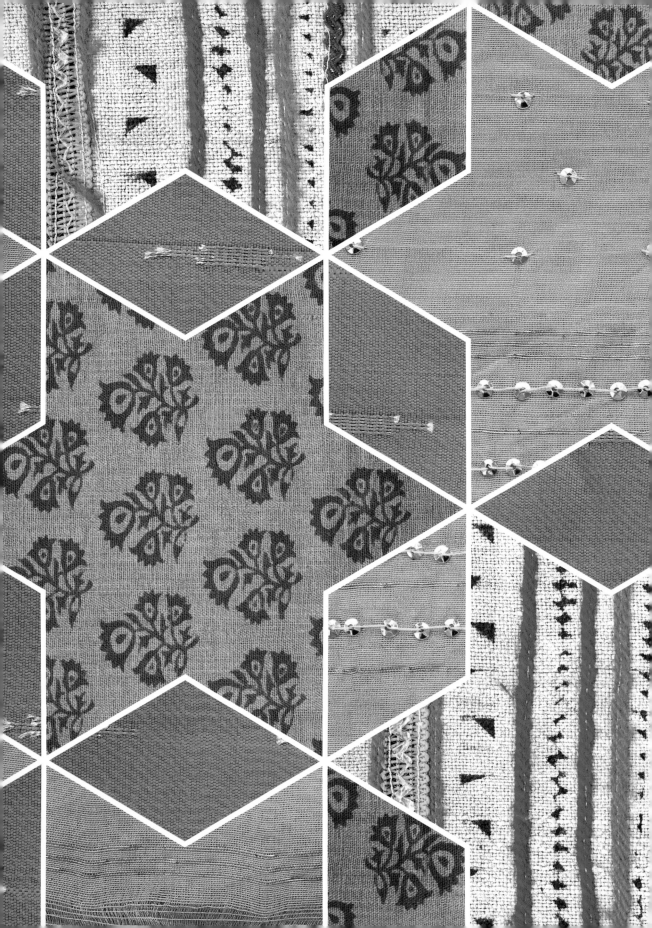

EASY
MEALS

CHILE PANEER

Paneer is an Indian cheese (imagine a softer, milder version of halloumi), and chile paneer is one of my all-time favorite curries. It's spicy, sweet, nourishing, and comforting. Best served with warm naan.

SERVES 4

1 cup (125 g) cornstarch

1 teaspoon chile powder

½ teaspoon salt

1 teaspoon pepper

1 lb 10 oz (750 g) paneer, chopped

vegetable oil, for frying

1 red onion, sliced

2 scallions, sliced

1 yellow pepper, sliced

3 red chiles, finely sliced

1 Turkish green chile (for crunch and color), finely sliced (optional)

1 teaspoon garam masala

½ teaspoon ground turmeric

½ teaspoon chile flakes

⅓ cup (75 ml) ketchup

⅓ cup (75 ml) hot sauce

⅓ cup (75 ml) soy sauce

TO SERVE

naan bread

fresh cilantro leaves

In a large bowl, mix together the cornstarch, chile powder, salt, and pepper. Add the paneer and mix, making sure all the pieces are well coated in the flour.

Heat a frying pan with enough oil to coat the base of the pan. Fry your paneer cubes in small batches, for 2 minutes on each side, making sure each side of the paneer cubes gets some color. They should be crispy and golden brown. Once all your paneer has been fried, remove it from the pan and set aside.

Add the red onion, scallions, peppers, and chiles to the pan and fry for 3 minutes, until they just start to soften. We want to keep them mostly crunchy.

Add the garam masala, turmeric, and chile flakes and cook for 2 minutes, until they become fragrant. Then stir in the ketchup, hot sauce, and soy sauce and cook for 4 minutes over medium heat. The sauce should be bubbling lightly, allowing the raw chile taste to cook out. Put your crispy paneer back into the pan and toss it in the sauce, making sure it's fully coated.

Serve with warm naan and a sprinkle of cilantro leaves.

DESI CHOW MEIN

Growing up, my mom always gave her own Pakistani spin to a simple stir-fry by adding her own spices and masala. Try this Desi chow mein and you might never want to cook it any other way again.

SERVES 4

1 tablespoon vegetable oil

1 lb 2 oz (500 g) boneless skinless chicken, diced

1 teaspoon paprika

½ teaspoon chile powder

½ teaspoon garam masala

¼ teaspoon mustard seeds

6 garlic cloves, grated

5½ oz (150 g) dried egg noodles

2 carrots, sliced

heaped 1 cup (100 g) sliced white cabbage

1 red pepper, sliced

1½ cups (100 g) sliced mushrooms

heaped 1 cup (80 g) snow peas

3½ tablespoons soy sauce

4 tablespoons hot sauce of your choice

2 tablespoons toasted sesame oil

salt

2 scallion greens, sliced

In a large wok or large nonstick pan, heat the oil and fry the chicken pieces until fully cooked and brown on all sides—this may take up to 12 minutes. Stir in all the spices and the garlic and cook for 3–4 minutes over medium heat, until fragrant. Transfer the chicken to a plate and set aside.

In a large bowl, soak the egg noodles in boiling water for 5 minutes until just soft. Set aside until ready to cook.

Add the carrots and cabbage to the wok or pan first (they take the longest to cook) and stir-fry for 2–3 minutes, then add the red peppers and mushrooms and stir-fry for another 2 minutes. Add a splash of water if the pan gets too dry.

Return the chicken to the pan and stir well, then add the snow peas just before adding the sauces and noodles.

Stir in both the sauces and the sesame oil, and toss in the noodles. Season with salt to taste.

Serve with a sprinkling of sliced scallion greens.

CRISPY FISH FILLET BURGERS

When we're having a burger night at home we don't often go for a fish option (it's usually chicken or beef), but you'll love this take on a certain popular fish fillet burger. And once you try these crunchy potato matchsticks, you'll be adding a handful to every sandwich you make.

SERVES 4

neutral oil, for deep-frying

9 oz (250 g) potatoes

2 cups (250 g) all-purpose flour

1 teaspoon chile powder

1 teaspoon garam masala

1 teaspoon ground turmeric

1 teaspoon salt

1 teaspoon black pepper

1 large egg

2¼ cups (250 g) dried breadcrumbs

4 cod fillets (or any firm white fish)

TO SERVE

4 burger buns

tartar sauce

lettuce leaves

cheese slices (optional)

Slice the potatoes into matchsticks, then rinse with cold water until the water runs clear, to remove the starch. Drain and pat with paper towels until completely dry.

Heat enough oil in a pot to deep-fry. It is hot enough when a small piece of bread sizzles immediately when you add it to the oil.

Fry the potato matchsticks in the hot oil in batches for 4–6 minutes, until lightly golden and crispy, then drain and set aside ready for assembling. Don't overfill the pan.

In a bowl, mix the flour with half the spices and the salt and pepper. In another bowl whisk an egg with the remaining half of each spice and a splash of water to make an egg wash. Place the breadcrumbs in a third bowl. Dip each fish fillet first into the seasoned flour, then into the egg, then into the breadcrumbs, making sure it is fully coated.

Fry the fish in two batches in the same oil as the potatoes for 6–8 minutes, until crispy.

Slice and toast your burger buns, and assemble with a spoonful of tartar sauce on each side of the bun, then some lettuce, followed by the fish fillet and a slice of cheese if you like, topped with a handful of crispy potato matchsticks.

ONE-POT SALMON AND RICE

This is the most recreated recipe of my viral Ramadan Recipe series online. It can be prepped and cooked in just 20 minutes. It is always a good idea to cook extra rice, since the leftovers are so useful in dishes like this one.

SERVES 4

1 tablespoon olive oil

6 garlic cloves, sliced

1 red onion, diced

2 teaspoons paprika

2 teaspoons chile powder

1 teaspoon cumin seeds

1 teaspoon salt

1 tablespoon honey

4 skinless salmon fillets

2¾ cups (500 g) day-old cooked rice (see page 22)

½ a lime

Preheat the oven to 425°F/220°C.

Put the oil, garlic, and onions into a roasting pan and season with half the spices and salt. Add a drizzle of honey and give it a good mix. Lay your salmon fillets on top and evenly sprinkle the rest of the spices and salt over the salmon. Place in the oven for 6 minutes.

After 6 minutes the salmon fillets will be halfway cooked. Remove the salmon from the pan, then add your cooked day-old rice and mix it into the onions. The rice will soak up all that flavor and caramelize at the bottom of the pan. Put your salmon fillets back on top, return the pan to the oven for another 6 minutes.

Serve with a squeeze of lime.

DYNAMITE SHRIMP

A simple dish of crispy shrimp, topped with a spicy dynamite sauce that you can make in just minutes. Serve these shrimp with rice for a quick lunch for two, or just as they are as an appetizer for four people.

SERVES 2, OR 4 AS AN APPETIZER

vegetable oil, for deep-frying

2 eggs

1 tablespoon soy sauce

1 tablespoon garlic granules

1 teaspoon chile powder

salt and black pepper

scant 1 cup (100 g) cornstarch

scant ½ cup (50 g) all-purpose flour

½ teaspoon sea salt

14 oz (400 g) jumbo shrimp, peeled and deveined

FOR THE SAUCE

½ cup (100 g) mayonnaise

2 tablespoons sriracha

2 tablespoons sweet chile sauce

1 tablespoon hot chile sauce (optional)

1 teaspoon soy sauce

½ teaspoon paprika

TO SERVE

sesame seeds

1 scallion, chopped

In a pot, heat enough oil to deep-fry. Once it just starts to smoke, turn it down to low-medium heat.

Whisk together the eggs, soy sauce, garlic granules, and chile powder, and season with salt and pepper. On a separate plate, combine the dry ingredients (cornstarch, flour, and sea salt) to make the flour dredge.

Coat each shrimp and in flour, then put it straight into the frying oil. Fry in batches for 2–3 minutes, until golden brown and crispy, turning them over occasionally so that they cook evenly. Drain on paper towels.

In a small bowl, mix together the ingredients for the dynamite sauce. Serve the shrimp with a generous spoonful of sauce over the top and finish with sesame seeds and chopped scallions.

CREAMY CHIPOTLE CHICKEN TACOS

These smoky tacos are a weeknight favorite, and chipotle chile paste has become a pantry staple for me. Just 1 teaspoon can transform an entire dish, infusing it with a punchy, rich, Mexican flavor.

SERVES 4

FOR THE TACOS

1 lb 10 oz (750 g) boneless skinless chicken

a splash of oil

1 teaspoon cumin seeds

½ teaspoon yellow mustard seeds

1 teaspoon Kashmiri chile powder

2 tablespoons chipotle chile paste

½ teaspoon chile flakes

salt and pepper

½ cup (125 ml) light cream

a handful of grated Cheddar

8 flour tortillas

3½ oz (100 g) pickled jalapeños (optional)

FOR THE SLAW

9 oz (250 g) red cabbage, thinly sliced

9 oz (250 g) white cabbage, thinly sliced

½ cup (100 g) mayonnaise

1 teaspoon mustard

chopped fresh cilantro

Chop your chicken into smaller-than-bite-size pieces and brown them in a hot pan with a splash of oil and the cumin seeds, mustard seeds, and chile powder.

Once the chicken has browned all over, add the chipotle chile paste, chile flakes, and a splash of water, and season with salt and pepper. Cook over low heat for 5 minutes, stirring occasionally.

Add the cream, plus a splash of water if the mixture is too dry, simmer for 5 minutes, then remove from the heat. Stir in the grated Cheddar. Once the cheese has melted, cover the pan with a lid to keep it warm while you make the slaw.

Put the sliced cabbage, mayonnaise, mustard, and chopped cilantro into a large mixing bowl. Season with salt and pepper and mix well so that all the cabbage is coated.

Heat a nonstick frying pan. Spoon your chicken onto one half of each tortilla, fold over, then toast in the pan for 3–4 minutes on each side, until crispy and slightly golden brown.

Scoop some slaw onto each taco, with some jalapeños, if you like, and enjoy.

SATAY CHICKEN & RICE

If you fancy introducing some new flavors into your Desi kitchen but don't have much time, try this one-pot satay chicken and rice. It's easy to throw together within 45 minutes, using pantry essentials like peanut butter and soy sauce.

SERVES 2–4

6 skin-on boneless chicken thighs

2 cups (400 g) risotto rice

3 cups (700 ml) water

6 garlic cloves, grated

3 tablespoons peanut butter

3½ tablespoons soy sauce

2 tablespoons crispy chile oil, plus extra to serve

1 tablespoon toasted sesame oil

2 scallions, sliced, to serve

Heat a large, deep nonstick frying pan. Once the pan is hot, place your chicken thighs skin side down and cook over medium heat for 15 minutes. You don't need any oil in the pan—fat is naturally released as the chicken cooks. Occasionally lift a piece to check on your chicken and make sure it is not burning.

Turn the chicken thighs over, cook for 10 minutes on this side, then remove from the pan.

Toast your rice in the chicken fat for 2 minutes, then add the water. Bring to a boil, then reduce the heat and cook, uncovered, over medium heat for 6 minutes.

Meanwhile, make the satay sauce. Mix together the grated garlic, peanut butter, soy sauce, chile oil, and sesame oil. Loosen with a splash of hot water if needed.

After 6 minutes your rice will be half cooked. Give it a stir, then put the chicken thighs on top of the rice and spoon your satay sauce all over. Cover with a lid and cook over low heat for 10 more minutes.

After 10 minutes, remove the lid and cook for 3 more minutes over very low heat to allow any extra moisture to evaporate. Garnish with chopped scallions and spoon over some extra chile oil if you like.

HARISSA CHICKEN & RICE

This is a go-to family dinner for us, and is especially popular on busy days because it all comes together quickly and easily. Harissa is a chile pepper spice paste commonly used in Middle Eastern and North African cooking—it comes in small jars and you can find it in most major supermarkets. Harissa has become a pantry staple for us!

SERVES 2–4

6 skin-on boneless chicken thighs

2 tablespoons harissa paste

2 tablespoons honey

2 cups (400 g) basmati rice, washed (see page 22)

generous 3 cups (750 ml) water

1 chicken bouillon cube, crumbled

1 teaspoon chile powder

1 teaspoon ground turmeric

sliced scallions, to serve

Heat a large, deep nonstick frying pan. Once the pan is hot, put in your chicken thighs skin side down and cook over medium heat for 15 minutes. You don't need any oil in the pan—the fat is naturally released as the chicken thighs cook. Occasionally lift a piece to check on your chicken and make sure it's not burning.

In a small bowl, mix together the harissa and honey. Add a splash of water to loosen, and spoon half this sauce onto your chicken while it is still skin side down.

Turn the chicken thighs over and spoon the remainder of your sauce all over the skin side of the chicken. Cover the pan and cook for 10 minutes on this side.

At this point your chicken is 80 percent cooked and will finish cooking with the rice. Remove the chicken thighs from the pan.

Add the rice and water to the pan and bring to a boil, then drop in your bouillon cube and spices. Reduce the heat, cover with a lid, and simmer for 8 minutes.

After 8 minutes, remove the lid and gently stir. Your rice should now be half cooked and a rich yellow in color. Place your chicken thighs on top and cover with a lid again. Cook for 8 minutes with the lid on the pan, then 2 minutes uncovered. This allows any extra moisture to evaporate in the final few minutes.

Finish with a sprinkling of sliced scallions.

BUTTER CHICKEN BURGER

Succulent grilled tandoori chicken breast, smothered in a rich butter chicken sauce, inside a sweet brioche bun. You've never had a burger like this before!

SERVES 4

FOR THE CHICKEN AND MARINADE

1 cup (250 g) whole-milk plain yogurt

6–8 garlic cloves, grated

1 thumb-size piece of ginger, grated

½ tablespoon garam masala

½ tablespoon ground cumin

½ tablespoon chile powder

¼ tablespoon ground cumin

½ teaspoon sea salt

4 small chicken breast fillets

FOR THE SAUCE

1 onion, finely diced

3 tablespoons ghee

1 star anise

1 cinnamon stick

4 black cloves

1 teaspoon cumin seeds

2 curry leaves

1 tablespoon tomato paste

½ tablespoon garam masala

½ tablespoon ground cumin

½ tablespoon chile powder

¼ tablespoon ground cumin

1 x 14 oz (400 g) can of tomatoes

1 tablespoon dried methi

sea salt

generous 1 cup (250 g) mayonnaise

handful of cilantro, chopped

TO SERVE

4 seeded brioche burger buns

lettuce, tomato slices, pickles

In a large bowl, mix the yogurt with the garlic, ginger, spices, and salt, then add the chicken and mix until well coated. Marinate in the fridge for at least an hour.

In a pan, soften the onions in the ghee over medium heat until completely caramelized. Add the star anise, cinnamon, cloves, cumin seeds, and curry leaves and cook for 2 minutes, until fragrant. Stir in the tomato paste, the ground spices, and a splash of water to make a spicy paste. Cook for 2 more minutes, then add the tomatoes and methi. Simmer for 20 minutes to make a masala, season with sea salt to taste, then set aside to cool. Once cool, stir the masala into the mayonnaise, together with the cilantro. Any leftover sauce will keep in the fridge for up to 5 days—it's great in sandwiches or with salads.

Grill or broil the chicken for 12–15 minutes on each side, until it is cooked through and begins to char on the outside.

Split and toast your brioche buns, then assemble the burgers with generous spoonfuls of sauce, the tandoori chicken, lettuce, tomatoes, and pickles.

BIRYANI-SPICED
CHICKEN BAKE

Craving biryani? Here's a one-pan chicken bake to get that quick fix in
45 minutes. This dish is full of all the rich flavors and aromatics of a biryani.

SERVES 4

1 cup (250 g) whole-milk plain yogurt

1 tablespoon olive oil

6–8 garlic cloves, grated

2 tablespoons Bombay Biryani Spice Mix (page 29)

1 teaspoon smoked paprika

1 teaspoon sea salt

1 lb 2 oz (500 g) baby potatoes

4 chicken legs or 8 drumsticks

chopped fresh cilantro, to serve

Preheat the oven to 425°F/220°C. Line a baking dish or roasting pan with parchment paper.

In a bowl mix the yogurt, olive oil, grated garlic, biryani spice mix, paprika, and sea salt.

Arrange the potatoes in the dish or pan. Coat the chicken in the marinade, then place each piece in the pan, leaving some space between them. Bake in the oven for 35–40 minutes until cooked through and slightly crispy on top.

Sprinkle with chopped cilantro, and serve.

BOMBAY CHICKEN BURGER

Bombay mix coating for fried chicken? Absolutely. This is Desi innovation at its finest, and what better way to use up leftover Bombay mix before it turns soggy. There are so many varieties of Bombay mix to choose from—from crispy sev to the classic hot Bombay mix—and you can use absolutely any kind you enjoy!

SERVES 4

neutral oil, for deep frying

2 teaspoons paprika

1 teaspoon chile powder

1 teaspoon chile flakes

1 teaspoon black pepper

½ teaspoon garlic granules

2 cups (250 g) all-purpose flour

2 eggs

3¼ cups (200 g) Bombay mix

2 chicken breasts, halved

TO SERVE

4 seeded brioche burger buns

mango chutney

mayonnaise

hot sauce

beefsteak tomatoes, sliced

shredded lettuce

Heat enough oil in a deep pan to deep-fry. It is hot enough when a small piece of bread sizzles immediately when you add it to the oil.

Meanwhile, in a bowl mix the spices with the flour. In a separate bowl whisk together the eggs until combined. Pour the Bombay mix onto a plate so that your chicken station is ready.

Dip each chicken breast fillet first into the flour, then into the egg, then into the Bombay mix. Really push the Bombay mix into the chicken to completely coat it.

When the oil is ready, fry the chicken for 12–15 minutes, keeping the chicken pieces spaced apart, so they don't stick together and turning them over occasionally so that they cook evenly. Once the meat is white and the juices run clear, it's fully cooked.

Assemble the burgers with toasted buns, mango chutney, sauces, tomato slices, and lettuce, and enjoy with a side of fries if you like (see pages 95 and 148 for Masala Fries and potato matchsticks).

DESI WHOLE ROAST CHICKEN

This is my idea of the perfect roast chicken, oozing with flavor, with crispy skin and juicy tender meat. It's simple, succulent, a family favorite quick dinner. I like to serve it with a green salad—it's an easy win that's hard to get wrong!

SERVES 4

1 large chicken, skin-on and spatchcocked (a butcher can also do this for you)

1 tablespoon butter, plus extra to grease

1 tablespoon oil

6–8 garlic cloves, grated

1 tablespoon brown sugar

1 tablespoon soy sauce

1 tablespoon paprika

2 teaspoons garam masala

2 teaspoons chile powder

2 teaspoons sea salt

1 teaspoon cumin seeds

1 red chile, sliced

2 scallions, sliced

Preheat the oven to 400°F/200°C.

Lay the chicken flat in a greased baking dish or roasting pan.

Melt the butter in the microwave, then add the oil, garlic, sugar, soy sauce, spices, and salt. Stir in the red chiles and scallions, then coat your chicken with this marinade.

Roast in the oven for 30 minutes (after 15 minutes, baste the chicken with the juices in the dish). After the 30 minutes, increase the heat to 475°F/240°C and cook for a further 8–10 minutes, to crisp up the skin.

Remove the chicken from the oven and let it rest for 10 minutes before serving. I like this with a green salad.

TAMARIND-GLAZED
CHICKEN THIGHS

Tamarind sauce when grilled is like Desi teriyaki. It's sweet, tangy, and rich in flavor. Use chicken thighs with skin for extra flavor and crispness.

SERVES 2–4

⅓ cup (75 ml) tamarind sauce

2 tablespoons tomato paste

1 tablespoon olive oil

1 tablespoon grated ginger

1 tablespoon grated garlic

1 bird's-eye chile, finely chopped

salt and pepper

½ teaspoon chile flakes

6 chicken thighs, skin on, scored

2 scallions, sliced

In a bowl mix the tamarind sauce, tomato paste, olive oil, ginger, and garlic. Add the chile, season well with salt and pepper, then add up to ½ teaspoon of chile flakes, according to your desired spice level.

Spread the marinade over your scored chicken thighs and leave in the fridge to marinate for a minimum of 2 hours, to allow the flavor to seep deep into the chicken.

Grill (or broil) on medium heat for around 12 minutes on each side, until fully cooked through. The juices should run clear, the top should be charred, and the skin crispy.

Serve over rice, sprinkled with scallions, with chutney on the side (see pages 18–19).

ALOO GOSHT

A simple Pakistani and Bangladeshi curry which directly translates as "potato meat." It's a soupier curry compared to others, and is typically served over rice to soak in all that spicy shorba (runny gravy).

SERVES 4–6

2 lb 4 oz (1 kg) mutton pieces, on the bone

2 tablespoons ghee

1 onion, sliced

1 tablespoon grated garlic

1 tablespoon grated fresh ginger

1 teaspoon chile powder

1 teaspoon garam masala

¾ teaspoon sea salt

½ teaspoon ground turmeric

½ teaspoon cumin seeds

¼ teaspoon mustard seeds

7 oz (200 g) tomatoes, chopped (fresh or canned)

4¼ cups (1 liter) water

14 oz (400 g) baby potatoes

a large handful of fresh cilantro, chopped

rice, to serve

In a Dutch oven or heavy pot, fry the mutton in the ghee until browned all over, then add the onions, garlic, and ginger. Cook for up to 10 minutes, until the onions have completely caramelized, then stir in the spices and salt. Cook for 2 more minutes, until the spices are fragrant.

Add the chopped tomatoes and enough water to cover the meat (about 4¼ cups/1 liter). Cover the pot, then simmer over low heat for a minimum of 2 hours. Add more water if needed.

Once the meat is tender, add the baby potatoes to the pot. Cook over medium heat with the lid off for 12–15 minutes, or until the potatoes are just tender.

Finish with the cilantro, and serve over rice.

SPAGHETTI KEEMA

This recipe inspired the name of my book. Many South Asian families grow up eating a Desified version of classic everyday meals. Keema is a dry, spicy ground meat curry, usually made using mutton. Mix this with a tomato sauce and serve it over spaghetti for a Desified version of the classic spaghetti bolognese.

SERVES 4–6

1 tablespoon olive oil

1 large red onion, finely chopped

1 teaspoon chile powder

1 teaspoon garam masala

1 teaspoon salt

½ teaspoon black pepper

½ teaspoon dried basil

1 tablespoon tomato paste

1 lb 10 oz (750 g) ground mutton, lamb, or beef

1 x 1 lb 2 oz (500 g) jar of tomato-based pasta sauce

4–6 x 3½ oz (100 g) portions dried spaghetti

1 oz (30 g) Parmesan, grated

fresh basil leaves, to serve

In a large nonstick sauté pan, soften your onions with the olive oil over medium heat. Once they're soft, add your spices, salt, and dried basil and cook for 2 minutes, until fragrant. Add a splash of water if needed. Add the tomato paste and stir until it well mixed. This concentrated masala makes up the base of your "bolognese" sauce.

Add the ground meat (mutton is preferred, but lamb or beef would work too). Brown the meat for 10–12 minutes, mixing continuously to ensure it doesn't burn. Again add a splash of water if needed.

Add the pasta sauce and season with salt to taste. Add ½ cup (125 ml) of water and bring to a boil, then reduce the heat and simmer gently with the lid on for 25–30 minutes.

Meanwhile, cook the spaghetti in a large pot of boiling water for 6–8 minutes, until just al dente (check your package instructions). Don't overcook the pasta—it's best it has a bit of bite, as it will cook further in the keema.

Using tongs, transfer the spaghetti directly from the pot of boiling water into the sauce and let it soak in the flavors of the keema for a couple of minutes.

Serve with a grating of Parmesan and a scattering of fresh basil leaves.

SPICY LAMB BURGERS

This is my Mediterranean-inspired lamb burger recipe. My key to making the most delicious burger is to use lots of finely chopped fresh mint and caramelized red onions.

SERVES 4

1 lb 2 oz (500 g) lean ground lamb

2 red onions

2 tablespoons olive oil

½ tablespoon chile flakes

½ tablespoon ground cumin

2 teaspoons chile powder

a handful of fresh mint, chopped

4 garlic cloves, grated

salt and black pepper

¼ of a cucumber

scant 1 cup (200 g) Greek yogurt

1 beefsteak tomato

4 burger buns

a large handful of arugula

Put the ground meat into a bowl. Finely chop your onions and sauté them in 1 tablespoon of the olive oil until completely caramelized. Add them to the meat, along with your spices, mint, and garlic. Season with salt and pepper.

Heat the other tablespoon of oil in your pan over medium heat. Shape the meat mixture into 4 burger patties and cook them for 6 minutes on each side.

Grate the cucumber into a bowl and add the yogurt. Season with black pepper.

Slice your tomatoes and open up your burger buns. Toast your burger buns for 2 minutes, until lightly golden and crispy.

Then assemble your buns with the cucumber yogurt, arugula, tomatoes, and lamb burgers.

SWEET
TREATS

ROSE TRES LECHES CAKE

The only problem with this cake is that it's so light and pillowy you end up eating your way through multiple slices in one sitting! My version of tres leches, or milk cake, is gently infused with rose syrup and topped with spoonfuls of silky whipped cream and lots of fresh strawberries.

SERVES 8+

1⅔ cups (200 g) all-purpose flour

1 teaspoon baking powder

1 cup (200 g) sugar

7 tablespoons (100 g) unsalted butter, plus extra to grease the pan

4 eggs

2½ tablespoons rose syrup, like Rooh Afza

2 cups (500 ml) whole milk

½ cup (125 g) evaporated milk

scant ½ cup (125 g) sweetened condensed milk

2 cups (500 ml) heavy cream

fresh strawberries, halved or quartered

cookie crumbs of your choice, to serve (optional)

Preheat your oven to 425°F/220°C, and grease a 9 x 13 inch (22 x 32 cm) baking pan.

In a large bowl, sift together the flour and baking powder. In a separate bowl, beat together the sugar and butter until light and fluffy. Then beat in the eggs, one at a time, and 1 tablespoon of the rose syrup. Stir in the flour until it's well combined and smooth. Pour the batter into the pan and bake in the oven for 25–30 minutes, or until a toothpick comes out clean.

In the meantime, prepare the milk glaze. Mix the milk, evaporated milk, and condensed milk together with another tablespoon of rose syrup. The milks should be well combined and light pink in color.

In a large bowl, using an electric mixer, whip the cream until it's fluffy and just holds its shape (don't over-whip). Divide the cream between 2 bowls. Add ½ tablespoon of rose syrup to one bowl and mix until pink in color. Spoon 2 layers of the whipped cream into a pastry bag, white on the bottom and pink on top. If you don't have a pastry bag, you can just use a spoon.

Once the cake has cooled to room temperature, use a fork to pierce holes all over it. Pour over the milk glaze and allow it to soak into the cake for a few minutes.

Pipe the cream all over the cake in your desired pattern. Decorate with fresh strawberries and finish with a sprinkling of cookie crumbs, if you like. Keep refrigerated until serving.

CHAI CHURROS

Churros are pieces of crispy fried dough with a soft middle. These are gently spiced with cinnamon and served alongside a chai-infused chocolate dip.

MAKES 6–8

1 cup (250 ml) whole milk

scant 1 cup (200 ml) water

3 tablespoons black tea leaves or 5 black tea bags

4 green cardamom pods

1½ tablespoons ground cinnamon

3 cups (350 g) all-purpose flour

vegetable oil, for frying

3½ oz (100 g) dark chocolate

1 cup (250 ml) Karak Chai (page 202)

½ cup (100 g) brown sugar

In a large pot, bring the milk and water to a boil. Add the black tea, cardamom pods, and 1 tablespoon of cinnamon, and simmer over low heat for 5 minutes to strengthen the tea flavor. Remove from the heat, strain the liquid, then gently stir in the flour until smooth. It should have the consistency of a thick batter and should hold its shape. Add extra flour if needed, and set aside to cool.

Heat enough oil for deep-frying in a large pot. It is hot enough when a small piece of bread sizzles immediately when you add it to the oil.

Prepare your pastry bag with a star-shaped tip and spoon in your churro batter once it is cool enough to handle.

Pipe lengths of about 4½–6 inches (12–15 cm) of batter into the oil, forming long "U" shaped churros. Fry for 3–4 minutes, or until golden and crisp, turning them over occasionally so that they cook evenly. Cook in small batches and be careful not to overcrowd the pot.

In a separate small saucepan, melt the dark chocolate with the karak chai. Pour into a small bowl for serving.

On a plate, combine the remaining cinnamon with the brown sugar. As you lift each churro out of the oil, roll it in the cinnamon sugar and place on a plate ready to serve, with the chocolate dip.

CARAMEL COOKIE TIRAMISÙ

Tiramisù is an Italian dessert traditionally made with espresso-dipped lady finger cookies (also known as savoiardi) topped with sweet mascarpone cream. This version uses those crunchy little Belgian cookies (speculoos) as well as the traditional lady fingers for a caramel twist.

SERVES 6–8

1¼ cups (300 ml) heavy cream

9 oz (250 g) mascarpone

2 tablespoons sugar

1 cup (250 ml) boiling water

2 tablespoons instant coffee granules

3½–5½ oz (100–150 g) lady finger cookies (approx. 15–20)

½ cup (120 g) caramelized cookie butter, like Biscoff

5½ oz (150 g) speculoos cookies, like Biscoff (about 19)

1 tablespoon cocoa powder

Put the cream into a large bowl and whisk using an electric mixer until it starts to thicken. Add the mascarpone and sugar, then whisk for a further 5–6 minutes until everything is combined and has the consistency of thick whipped cream.

In a shallow dish, mix the boiling water with the coffee granules and leave to cool for a few minutes. Soak the lady finger cookies two at a time, for a few seconds on each side. They should be nicely soaked but not soggy. Layer them in a 7 x 12 inch (19 x 30 cm) rectangular or oval baking dish until the entire bottom layer is covered. This might use up to 20 lady fingers.

Spoon over half the cream mixture and gently spread it using the back of a spoon. Drizzle over 3 tablespoons of biscoff cookie butter (warm it in the microwave for 20 seconds if necessary, to make it easier to drizzle).

Now soak your speculoos cookies in the coffee mixture for a couple of seconds and layer them on top, covering the entire tiramisù.

Spoon over the remaining cream and spread it level, using the back of a spoon. It's okay if it isn't perfect.

To finish, drizzle over the remaining cookie butter, then dust all over with cocoa powder.

GAJAR KA HALWA

Gajar ka halwa is a simple classic Punjabi dessert made by simmering grated carrots with milk, cardamom, and sugar. It's best served hot, with a side of cool Pistachio Kulfi (page 186).

SERVES 6+

2 lb 4 oz (1 kg) carrots, peeled and grated

¾ cup (100 g) pistachios

2 tablespoons ghee

6 green cardamom pods

4¼ cups (1 liter) milk

1¼ cups (240 g) organic sugar

Pistachio Kulfi (page 186) or your favorite ice cream, to serve

Start by peeling and grating the carrots, either by hand or using the grating blade of a food processor.

In a large pot, lightly toast the pistachios until they become fragrant. Then remove them from the pot and set aside, ready for garnishing later.

Melt 1 tablespoon of ghee in the same pot, then increase the heat to high and fry the cardamom pods for 2 minutes, until they become fragrant. Add the carrots and sauté for up to 10 minutes, to remove a lot of the moisture. Add the milk and bring to a boil, then reduce the heat to medium and simmer for 40–50 minutes, stirring occasionally.

Once the halwa has reduced and thickened, stir in the sugar. Some moisture will be released, so increase the heat until it thickens up again to your desired consistency.

Melt the remaining tablespoon of ghee in a small pan and drizzle a little melted ghee over each serving of halwa. Garnish with the toasted pistachios and a scoop of pistachio kulfi or your favorite ice cream.

CHAI CRÈME BRÛLÉE

I always thought crème brûlée was a super tricky technical dessert to make, but I was wrong! Impress your family and dinner party guests with this super simple chai crème brûlée. Most of us won't have kitchen blowtorches on hand, but you can achieve that iconic crunchy top by placing your sugared crème brûlée under the broiler for a couple of minutes.

MAKES 6

1 large egg

4 large egg yolks

½ cup (100 g) sugar (plus 1 tablespoon per serving)

3 cups (700 ml) heavy cream

3 black tea bags

4 green cardamom pods

1 teaspoon ground cinnamon

1 teaspoon vanilla extract

Preheat your oven to 400°F/200°C.

In a large bowl, beat the egg, egg yolks, and sugar until just combined. Heat the cream in a saucepan until it's just boiling, then add the tea bags, cardamom pods, and cinnamon. Leave to cool for 15 minutes.

Gradually pour the cream into the eggs and whisk gently until combined. Then stir in the vanilla.

Create a bain-marie by placing 6 ramekins in a deep baking dish and filling with boiling water to come at least halfway up the sides of the ramekins. Pour the custard into the ramekins until almost full, then bake in the oven for 35–40 minutes, until set. Chill in the fridge until firm.

To serve, sprinkle 1 tablespoon of sugar on top of each ramekin and either heat under a hot broiler for 2 minutes or use a kitchen blowtorch to evenly caramelize the sugar. Allow to set for 1 minute until the sugar hardens, then serve.

PISTACHIO KULFI

Kulfi is Indian ice cream, thicker and richer than regular ice cream. It's made by boiling and reducing milk, then flavoring it with nuts, spices, or syrups. Some popular flavors include mango, pistachio, and rose.

SERVES 6–8 DEPENDING ON THE SIZE OF YOUR MOLDS

6 green cardamom pods

1⅔ cups (200 g) pistachios

1 x 14 oz (396 g) can of sweetened condensed milk

1 x 12 fl oz (354 ml) can of evaporated milk

1¼ cups (300 ml) heavy cream

1 teaspoon vanilla extract

In a hot frying pan, toast the cardamom pods for 3–4 minutes until fragrant. Allow them to fully cool, then grind them using a coffee grinder or a mortar and pestle and set aside. Do the same with the pistachios.

In a large pot, bring both milks and the cream to a boil. Stir in the ground cardamom pods and most of the ground pistachios (reserving about a quarter of the ground pistachios for the garnish), then simmer for 15 minutes, stirring occasionally. Turn off the heat and stir in the vanilla extract. Allow to cool completely.

Once cool, pour into kulfi popsicle molds (you could also use plastic cups or yogurt containers). Insert the sticks, if using, and freeze for 8–10 hours or overnight.

To serve, hold the molds in your hands or under warm water for a couple of seconds and remove the kulfi from the molds, turning them out onto a plate. Sprinkle with the reserved ground pistachios and enjoy straight away.

KHEER

Kheer is a slow-cooked Indian rice pudding gently flavored with cardamom and rose. This creamy pudding can be served hot or cold at any time of day.

SERVES 4–6

4¼ cups (1 liter) whole milk

10 green cardamom pods

scant ½ cup (75 g) basmati rice, washed (see page 22)

¼ cup (50 g) sugar

2 teaspoons rose water or 1 teaspoon rose syrup like Rooh Afza

scant ½ cup (50 g) pistachios

⅔ cup (50 g) flaked almonds

Bring the milk to a boil in a large pot, then add the cardamom pods and simmer over low heat for 5 minutes to release their flavor. Wash and add the rice and increase the heat to medium. Cover with a lid and cook for 25 minutes, stirring occasionally, until completely cooked and slightly mushy.

Stir in the sugar and continue cooking until the rice breaks down further into a thick batter-like consistency. Once it reaches your desired thickness, turn off the heat.

Stir in the rose water or syrup and allow to cool slightly before serving.

In a nonstick pan, toast your pistachios and flaked almonds for a few minutes until fragrant and the almonds turn lightly golden brown.

Serve in bowls, either hot or cold, and finish with a sprinkle of toasted nuts.

CHOCOLATE CAKE RUSKS

Cake rusks are twice-baked slices of cake with a crunchy, snappy texture. They're a South Asian household essential and are served alongside a hot cup of chai. During Ramadan, they're often eaten at Suhoor for a quick breakfast, with a hot cup of tea.

MAKES 10–12

½ cup (120 g) margarine

⅔ cup (120 g) sugar

2 large eggs

1 cup (120 g) all-purpose flour

½ cup (50 g) unsweetened cocoa powder

1 teaspoon baking powder

1 teaspoon vanilla extract

Preheat your oven to 425°F/220°C. Line an 8 x 8 inch (20 x 20 cm) square cake pan or a rectangular baking pan of similar size with parchment paper.

Using an electric mixer, beat together the margarine and sugar in a large bowl, until light and creamy. Whisk in 1 egg at a time and beat again until the mixture is smooth and creamy. Gradually sift in the flour, cocoa powder, and baking powder until completely combined. Finally stir in the vanilla extract.

Pour the batter into your prepared pan and bake for 30 minutes, until light golden on top and a toothpick comes out clean.

Once you've removed the cake from the oven, reduce the temperature to 350°F/180°C.

Allow the cake to cool for 15 minutes, then slice it into even sized rectangles with a thickness of 1 in (2½ cm). Arrange the slices on a baking sheet and bake for 10 minutes on each side, until dark golden brown.

Finally, allow the cake rusks to cool completely and serve with a hot cup of Masala or Karak Chai (pages 198 and 202).

KARAK COOKIES

These soft chewy cookies have all the flavors of a cup of Karak Chai (page 202).
Lightly spiced and moreish, bake a bunch to share with friends and family!

MAKES 10–15

2 sticks and 2 tbsp (250 g) unsalted butter

¾ cup (150 g) white sugar

¾ cup (150 g) light brown sugar

2 eggs

2 teaspoons ground cinnamon

1 teaspoon ground cardamom

1 teaspoon ground ginger

½ teaspoon black pepper

2 cups (250 g) all-purpose flour

1 teaspoon baking powder

scant 1 cup (150 g) milk chocolate chips

Start by melting your butter over low heat until it becomes dark golden brown—this could take up to 10 minutes, so be careful not to burn the butter. As soon as it goes golden brown, remove it from the heat and set it aside to cool.

In a large bowl, using an electric mixer, cream the brown butter and both sugars together until smooth and creamy. Crack in the eggs one at a time and whisk again after each addition until combined. Stir in your spices and fold in the flour and baking powder, followed by the chocolate chips. Mix until it forms a dough, then cover and chill in the fridge for at least 2 hours.

Before baking, preheat your oven to 475°F/240°C.

Depending on how big you want your cookies, divide the dough into 10–15 even-sized pieces. Shape them into balls, then gently squash them into thick discs between your hands. Place on lined baking sheets at least 3 inches (8 cm) apart.

Bake for 10–12 minutes, then cool for 10 minutes and serve!

CHAI AND CAKE RUSK CHEESECAKE

Cake rusks and a fresh cup of chai is a go-to after-dinner treat in my household. I decided to combine this perfect pairing into a delicious no-bake chai and rusk cheesecake. It's made with a cake rusk crust topped with chai-infused cream.

SERVES 6+

1¼ cups (300 ml) heavy cream

2⅔ cups (600 g) cream cheese

½ cup (50 g) confectioners' sugar

1 tablespoon masala chai spice mix or 1 masala chai packet

1 lb 2 oz (500 g) store-bought cake rusks

2 sticks and 2 tbsp (250 g) unsalted butter

⅔ cup (75 g) pistachios, crushed

Put the heavy cream in a large bowl and whip, using an electric mixer, for 2–3 minutes, until it's just thick enough to hold its peaks. Add the cream cheese, confectioners' sugar, and masala chai spice mix, and whisk again until combined.

Use a food processor to blend the cake rusks into crumbs. Alternatively place the rusks in a ziplock bag and smash them into crumbs using a rolling pin. Melt the butter in a microwaveable bowl, then stir the melted butter into the cake rusk crumbs.

Pour the crumbs into a 8 x 8 inch (20 x 20 inch) square baking dish (or a rectangular dish of similar size) and flatten it to form the base of the cheesecake. Place in the fridge for at least 30 minutes.

Once the base has set, spoon dollops of the cream cheese mixture on top and spread it out using the back of a spoon. Finish with a sprinkle of pistachios and leave in the fridge until ready to serve.

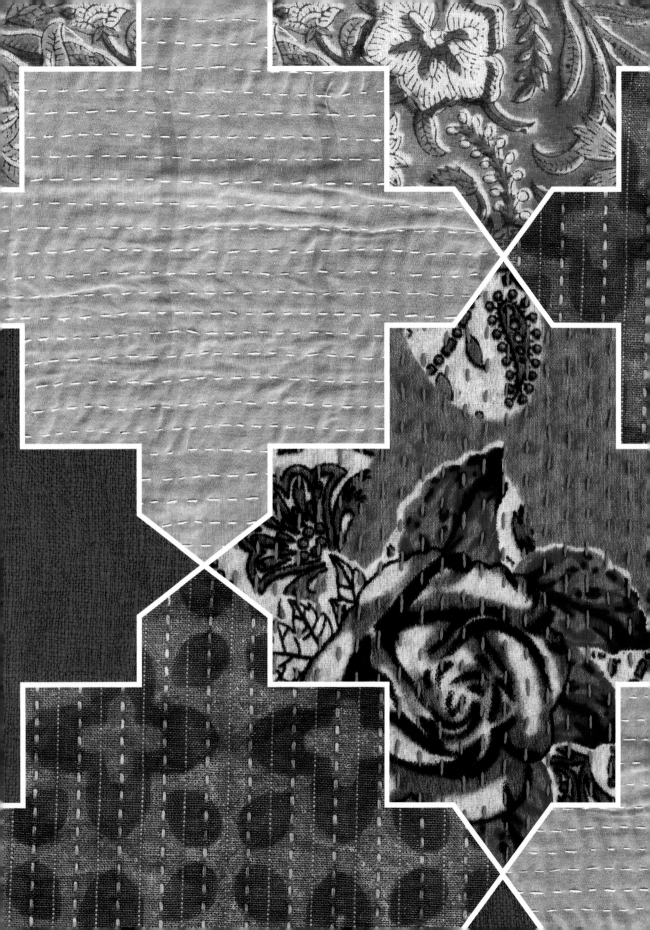

DRINKS

MASALA CHAI

Think of Masala Chai as Karak Chai's older sister (see page 202). She's spicier, stronger, and punchier. If you enjoy a spiced latte you will love this.

MAKES 4 TEA GLASSES

6 green cardamom pods

4 black peppercorns

1 teaspoon ground ginger

1 cinnamon stick

2 cups (500 ml) water

2 cups (500 ml) whole milk

3 tablespoons black tea leaves or 5 black tea bags

⅓ cup (100 g) sweetened condensed milk

In a small nonstick pan, toast all your spices for a few minutes until their aroma fills your kitchen.

In a small saucepan, bring the water and milk to a boil.

Add your toasted spices and black tea, remove from the heat, and let them steep for 5 minutes.

Now add the condensed milk and bring to a boil.

Remove from the heat and let the bubbles settle, then put back on the heat and bring it to a boil again. Keep doing this for 5 minutes, until the masala chai has deepened in color and flavor. It should be a rich caramel color.

Serve this using a tea strainer, and enjoy hot with a sweet treat or snack.

KASHMIRI PINK CHAI

Kashmiri chai, also known as pink chai or noon chai, is unique and my all-time favorite tea. Unlike all other teas, it is traditionally drunk salty, though nowadays it is sweetened to suit the modern taste. It is best served with a sweet pastry known as bakhar hani, to balance the salty tea.

MAKES 8 TEA GLASSES

4¼ cups (1 liter) water

6–8 green cardamom pods

1 cup (75 g) Kashmiri black tea leaves

1 teaspoon baking soda

1 cup (250 g) ice

TO SERVE

2 cups (500 ml) whole milk

salt, to taste

sugar, to taste (optional)

In a small saucepan, bring the water to a boil.

Crush the cardamom pods between your fingers and add them to the water along with the tea leaves. Let this boil for 30 minutes.

Add the baking soda—this reacts with the tea and will help give a vibrant pink color to the final drink. Then add the ice and 1 cup (225 ml) of cold water.

Continue boiling on a high heat for 20 minutes, while aerating it by taking a ladleful of tea at a time, lifting it to around 20 inches (50 cm) above the pan, then streaming it back into the tea. The longer you do this for, the better. You should see the color of the tea turn to a rich copper color. This black tea (kawa) can now be strained, cooled, and stored in the fridge for up to 2 weeks.

To prepare the tea for drinking, bring the milk to a boil in a separate pan, then add 1 cup (225 ml) of kawa. Add a sprinkle of salt (and sugar if you like), and serve hot.

KARAK CHAI

Karak chai is a rich and milky black tea infused with spices such as cardamom and cinnamon. It's truly comforting, and can be enjoyed at any time of the day but especially in the evening with a sweet treat.

MAKES 4 TEA GLASSES

2 cups (500 ml) water

2 cups (500 ml) whole milk

1 cinnamon stick, halved

4 green cardamom pods

3 tablespoons black tea leaves or 5 black tea bags

scant ½ cup (100 ml) sweetened condensed milk

In a saucepan, bring the water and milk to a boil.

Add the cinnamon, cardamom pods, and black tea, and remove from the heat to steep for 5 minutes.

Add the condensed milk and bring it back to a boil.

Remove from the heat and let the bubbles settle, then put it back on the heat and bring it to a boil again. Keep doing this for 5 minutes, until the karak chai has deepened in color and flavor. It should be a rich caramel color.

Pour through a tea strainer into tea glasses, and enjoy hot with a sweet treat or snack.

CARDAMOM ROSE LATTE

This one is especially for the coffee lovers. My brother Zayyan is a big coffee fan, and he often experiments in the kitchen to make new flavors of latte. He leaves behind a big mess but a delicious coffee. Try this indulgent milky latte infused with rose and cardamom, inspired by my brother.

SERVES 2

2 cups (500 ml) oat milk, or milk of your choice

6 green cardamom pods

2 teaspoons rose syrup like Rooh Afza

2–4 teaspoons instant coffee granules

condensed milk, to sweeten

Pour 1 cup (250 ml) oat milk into each mug. Then pinch the cardamom pods to release their flavor and add 3 to each mug. Place in the microwave for up to 2 minutes, until hot (keep an eye on it and stir halfway through).

Stir 1 teaspoon of rose syrup and 1–2 teaspoons of coffee granules (to taste) into each mug. Mix well until smooth, and finish with condensed milk to sweeten the latte to your desired taste.

Enjoy with a sweet treat.

ROOH AFZA DHOOD

Rooh Afza is a sweet concentrated rose syrup and is a staple in Desi and Arab households, particularly during Ramadan. It is often diluted in water or milk as a refreshing drink to open your fast with. Jazz up a simple glass of Rooh Afza dhood by adding soaked basil seeds and pieces of fresh strawberry. Enjoy at Iftar, with dates to break your fast.

SERVES 2

2 teaspoons basil seeds (tukmaria)

2 tablespoons Rooh Afza
(rose syrup)

2 cups (500 ml) whole milk

⅓ cup (50 g) chopped strawberries

In a small bowl, soak the basil seeds in 1 cup (250 ml) of water for up to 20 minutes, until they expand, then drain and set aside.

Stir the rose syrup into the milk and serve in glasses over ice. Add basil seeds and diced strawberries to each glass and enjoy chilled.

MANGO LASSI

This famous drink is essentially a more delicious (Desified) smoothie.
It is creamy, sweet, refreshing, and perfect to open your fast with,
or drink alongside a hot spicy curry.

SERVES 2

1 large ripe mango, diced, or
4 tablespoons mango pulp

⅔ cup (150 g) whole-milk plain
yogurt

2 cups (500 ml) whole milk

1 tablespoon honey, to sweeten
(optional)

½ teaspoon ground cinnamon

ice, to serve (optional)

Put the mango or mango pulp, yogurt, and milk into a blender, and blend until just smooth. Taste for sweetness—depending on the mango season you may need a dash of honey to sweeten the lassi. If you're using mango pulp rather than fresh mango, you most likely will not need any additional sweetener.

Add the cinnamon for warmth, then blend for a few seconds until combined.

Pour into your glasses and serve cold. Store in the fridge and serve cold, adding ice just before serving if you like.

ROSE NIMBU PANI

This nimbu pani (which translates as lemon water) is sweetened with rose syrup for a beautiful concoction of colors and flavors. The intense sweetness of rose syrup is balanced by fresh limes and black salt, which is readily available in most South Asian food stores.

SERVES 2

juice of 1 lime

2 cups (500 ml) water

2 tablespoons rose syrup like Rooh Afza

½ teaspoon kala namak (Indian black salt), or to taste

ice, to serve

1 bunch of fresh mint

Put the lime juice, water, and rose syrup into a jug and mix well. Then add the kala namak, a pinch at a time, until you reach your desired balance of flavors.

Serve in glasses, over ice. Pinch the mint leaves between your fingers to release their flavor, and add around 10 leaves to each glass (or you can put them directly in the jug).

LYCHEE MIRCH MOCKTAIL

Who says mocktails have to be boring? This is not your average mocktail and it's not for the faint-hearted! Try something daring with this infusion of sweet lychee and hot red chiles.

SERVES 4

1 x 20 oz (560 g) can of lychees in syrup

2 cups (500 ml) lychee juice

1 cup (250 ml) tonic water

1 tablespoon grated fresh ginger

1 cup (250 ml) water

1 red chile, sliced

Drain the can of lychees, saving the syrup!

Stir together a scant ½ cup (100 ml) of lychee syrup (from the can), the lychee juice, tonic water, and ginger. Taste and gradually add up to 1 cup (250 ml) of water to dilute to your taste.

Serve in glasses, over ice. Garnish each glass with a couple of thin slices of red chile and a pitted lychee.

STRAWBERRY
FALOODA BUBBLE TEA

Falooda is traditionally a chilled milky pudding with a sweet base, layered with basil seeds, vermicelli, fruit jello, and nuts. This strawberry falooda drink is a cross between a classic falooda and bubble tea.

SERVES 4

4 teaspoons basil seeds (tukmaria)

3½ oz (100 g) wheat vermicelli

boiling water

¼ cup (50 g) sugar

generous 1 cup (200 g) tapioca pearls

4 black tea bags

4¼ cups (1 liter) whole milk

2 tablespoons Rooh Afza (rose syrup)

TO SERVE

ice

1 cup (150 g) chopped strawberries

vanilla ice cream

Soak the basil seeds in 2 cups (500 ml) of water for 20 minutes, then drain and set aside.

Cook the vermicelli in boiling water according to the package directions until soft, then drain. Set aside.

Make a syrup by putting the sugar and 3½ tablespoons of water into a small pot over medium heat. Gently simmer until the sugar dissolves, then remove from the heat and leave to cool.

Carefully drop the tapioca pearls into a pot of boiling water and simmer over medium heat for 6–8 minutes, depending on how soft you want them. Drain and rinse under cold water. Once cool, stir the tapioca into the sugar syrup.

Steep the tea bags in 3 cups (750 ml) of boiling water for up to 10 minutes to make strong tea. Then leave to cool.

To serve, place a little ice into 4 tall glasses. Divide the tapioca mixture among the glasses, pour a generous 1 cup (250 ml) of milk into each glass, then stir ½ tablespoon of rose syrup into each one. Mostly fill up each class with tea (leaving some space at the top), then spoon in some basil seeds, vermicelli, and fresh strawberries.

Finish with a spoonful of ice cream and serve.

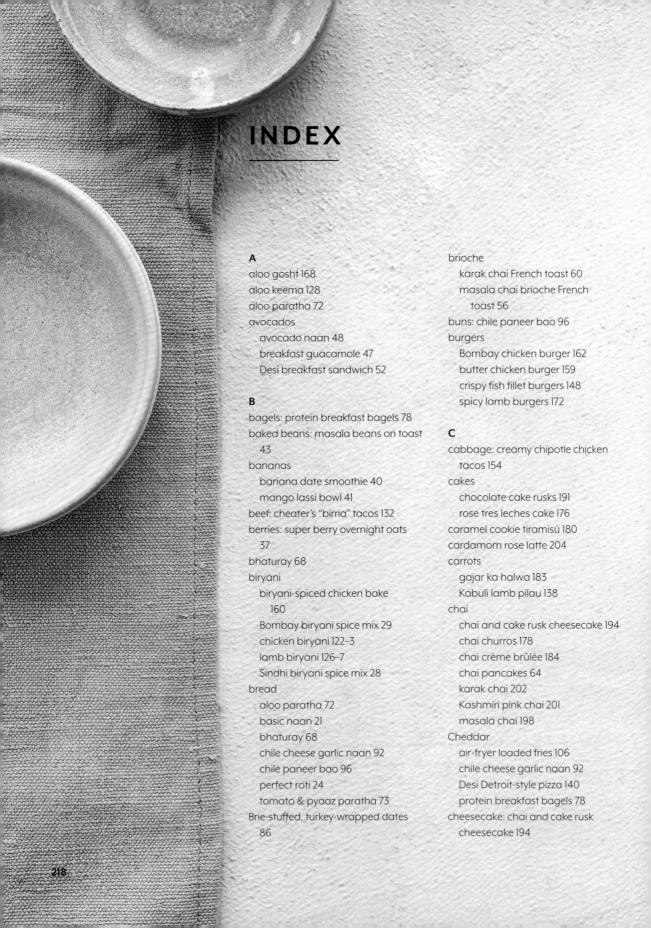

INDEX

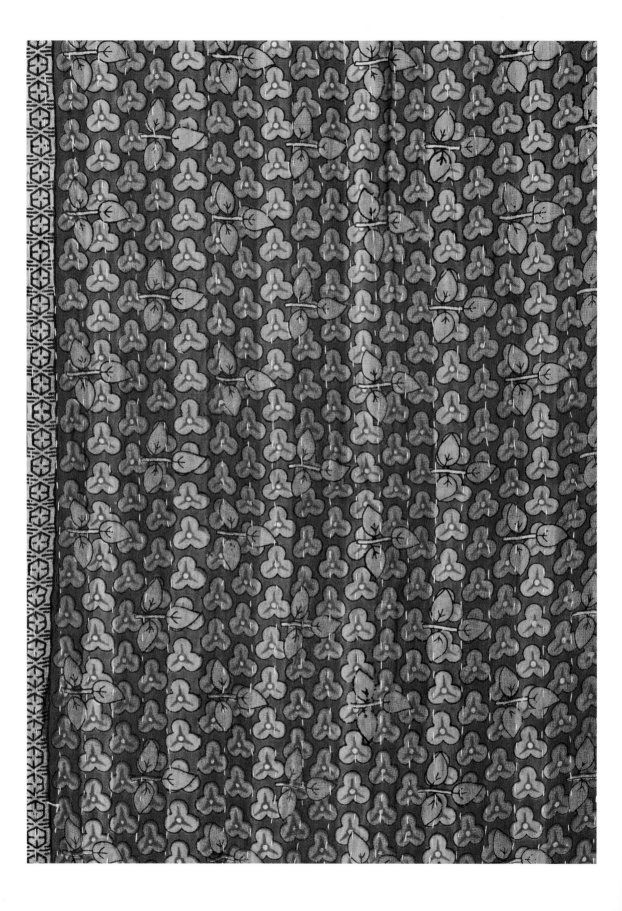

ACKNOWLEDGMENTS

First and foremost, thank you to my family. To my mom for being the entire inspiration for this book—thank you for allowing me to follow you around the kitchen and for letting me be tied to your waist to learn the art of your Pakistani food; for teaching us our culture through food; and for Desifying absolutely everything we ate. To my dad for always pushing me to follow my passion for food, for forcing me out of my comfort zone and into cooking competitions, and for taking me to the fishmonger at age 11 so I could learn how to gut a fish. Thank you to my siblings, Sara and Zayyan, for all the late-night snack experiments in the kitchen, for eating absolutely everything I cook, and for responding with "Hmm, nice" every single time I asked for feedback.

To my agents: Fadzi for completely leaning into every crazy idea I have and being the organized momager I need in life. To Silé for believing in me and seeing my vision.

Thank you to everyone at Octopus. To Natalie, my editor, for taking on this project with so much enthusiasm. Thank you to Alex for making sense of my words, and to Juliette for getting our visions on paper so amazingly.

A very special thanks to my shoot family: Sam, Charlotte, and co. None of this would be possible without you. Thank you for guiding me and answering every ridiculous question I had. Thanks for creating and shooting my recipes so beautifully and generally just being a joy to work with.

Thank you to my best friend for giving me the harsh feedback I needed, for telling me when my recipe test is absolute rubbish, for keeping me completely grounded in life, and continually supporting me through every challenge, and for being my biggest cheerleader and showing up at every occasion.

A final thank you goes to my audience—whether you've been following me from day one or if you only recently discovered my page. Although we may interact through a digital screen, I appreciate the support from every single one of you.

First American edition published in 2024 by

Interlink Books
An imprint of Interlink Publishing Group, Inc.
46 Crosby Street
Northampton, MA 01060
www.interlinkbooks.com

Published simultaneously in Great Britain by Hamlyn, an imprint of
Octopus Publishing Group Ltd, an Hachette UK Company

Library of Congress Cataloging-in-Publication data available
ISBN 978-1-62371-117-7

Printed and bound in China

10 9 8 7 6 5 4 3 2 1

Editorial Director: Natalie Bradley
US Edition Editor: Leyla Moushabeck
US Edition Proofreader: Jennifer McKenna
Senior Editor: Alex Stetter
Art Director: Juliette Norsworthy
Designer: Geoff Fennel
Photography: Charlotte Nott-Macaire
Home Economist: Sam Dixon
Props Stylist: Hannah Wilkinson
Production Manager: Caroline Alberti